VIEW OF SOUTH BERSTED CHURCH AND VICARAGE HOUSE.

Dean & Munday, Lithographers, Threadneedle St.

THE BOGNOR GUIDE,

CONTAINING

THE HISTORY OF BOGNOR,

AND

THE HISTORY AND ANTIQUITIES

OF

SEVERAL ADJOINING PARISHES,

INCLUDING

AN ACCOUNT OF GOODWOOD,

Arundel Castle, &c. &c.

AND

THE ROMAN REMAINS

AT

BIGNOR.

PETWORTH:
PRINTED BY JOHN PHILLIPS.

1838.

BOGNOR, I love, when summer heats prevail,
Around thy coast to wander; and inhale
The breeze, that blustering from the briny main,
Gives health and vigour to the rural swain;
Or, when the storm lies hid, my limbs to lave
(Not too adventurous) in the limpid wave.
Or else I love, at mornings early dawn,
To brush the dews that glitter o'er the lawn,
Whilst, from yon eastern hill, Apollo glides,
And waves his golden banners o'er the tides,
Gilds the dark rocks, illumes the dazzling main,
And spreads a thousand blessings o'er the plain!

CONTENTS.

A GUIDE, &c.

A GUIDE, &c.

CHAPTER I.

Containing a conjecture as to the Origin of the name of Bognor.

WHEN the Northern tribes of Barbarians came over to the shores of Britain on their predatory excursions, it was frequently their practice, in the pride of conquest, to give to the places they subdued a name corresponding with their own. For instance, we find that when the three sons of Ælla, named Cymen, Cissa and Wencheling came from Saxony, and landed at or near West-wittering, in Chichester Harbour, the first named chief called the territory on which he landed Cymen-ore or Cymen-shore; and there is to this day in that district a tract of land called Cumnore; an appellation clearly and sufficiently distinct to denote its derivation from Cymen-ore. As to Cissa, or Chissa, we well know that the term Chichester (the Regnum of the Romans) is compounded of the words *Cissa* and *cæstre;* and that Cissa reigned in that city, as sovereign of Sussex, or Suth-sex for many years. What became of Wencheling does not appear. In this way, it is not too bold to conjecture, that some other German chief, with his inharmonious name *Bogen*, became the conqueror of the Bognor shore and gave it the appellation of Bogen-ore—for the latter is exactly the name given to the place in ancient deeds and other documents, as the editor of this work has frequently experienced.

BOGNOR was formerly much more extensive than it now is. The general opinion is that the Rocks, now seen at low water, were anciently the Southern Boundary. Before the intended invasion of England by the Spanish Armada, the Government of Spain contrived to have surveys and maps made of the whole Southern Coast of England, and the Rocks of Bognor are therein laid down as very near the Cliff. In deeds of the date just mentioned, viz. that of Elizabeth, which are still extant, and in the hands of several individuals, who were purchasers of property under the will of Sir Richard Hotham, *the Southern* Boundary of property in Bognor now overflown by the sea is described to be "The Common of Bognor," which was an extensive tract of land lying in common, over which the proprietors had a right of pasture for a certain number of beasts, denominated leazes, but these rights are now become extinct; and, by operation of law, were merged in the inheritance in consequence of Sir Richard having purchased the manor to which they were appendant.

CHAPTER II.

The ancient History of Bognor, and of the parish of South Bersted, of which it is part.

THE parish, of which the town of Bognor now constitutes so considerable a portion, was formerly part of the ancient parish of Pagham, in former times denominated Pagen-ham, probably from its being then the abode of persons chiefly pagans, not yet converted to christianity like their neighbours, the inhabitants of Selsey, who, under Wilfride, the Bishop of Northumbria, at a very early period, viz. about 687, embraced that religion. Pagham, at the time of the conquest, was the hundred of the district according to the division of Alfred, and is so described in the "Domesdei boke" compiled by the conqueror; and is therein described as "The Territory of the Archbishop," within whose peculiar jurisdiction both Pagham and Southbersted still are. But Southbersted, including Bognor, have for many years past been detached from Pagham. Still, the Vicar of the latter place had the tithes of geese in Bognor then amounting to 2s. 8d. per annum!—; and if the Common of Bognor had been preserved from destruction by the sea, those tithes would perhaps have been now of considerable value. As it is, they are never thought of.

The separation of Southbersted from Pagham, and its conversion into a parish of itself, arose probably from the erection of the present Church, the consecration of which took place on the 23rd. of April, 1405, when two acres of land and more, were granted to the benefice, "but saving the "Right of the Mother Church of Pagham."(*a*) Before the year last mentioned, viz. in 1327, two chapels, one in "North Burghestede" dedicated to the Holy Cross, and another in "Bogenore," dedicated to Saint Bartholomew, and both declared to be Dependencies of Pagham, were in existence, but they have long since disappeared, and their scites are unknown.

(*a*) The commission to consecrate the Church is to be found in the Registry of the Dean and Chapter of Chichester.

CHAPTER III.

Modern History of Bognor.

Bognor, as a place for bathing, was founded by Sir Richard Hotham, a wealthy knight, who in a long course of successful commercial speculations, amassed a large fortune; and happening to visit this part of the Sussex coast, conceived the design of making Bognor, which was then occupied by a few farmers and fishermen, a place of fashionable resort in the bathing season. To accomplish this purpose, he began by purchasing the principal part of the lands, particularly those in the immediate vicinity of the sea-shore, in which purchases he was most essentially assisted by the persevering assiduity and activity of the Rev. Thomas Durnford, then vicar of the parish, with whom he contracted a close and intimate acquaintance*.

Having thus judiciously secured the sole proprietorship of the principal part of the building scites, Sir Richard commenced the erection of houses†. *Bognor Lodge*, lately the seat of Sir John Harington, Bart. but now the property of Mr. Pearson; *Hothampton Place; East Row; Bersted Lodge*, then called Chapel House;

* Sir Richard Hotham was knighted by George III. on occasion of carrying up to the throne an address on the birth of a prince. He was then Member of Parliament for the Borough of Southwark, having successfully opposed Mr. Thrale at the election for that borough.

† The worthy knight occupied first Bognor Lodge and afterwards Chapel House. The latter after his death was purchased by the late unfortunate Sir Thomas Troubridge, Bart. and subsequently became the property of Thomas Smith, Esq. and now belongs to Mrs. Smith, his widow.

Dome House,* and the houses adjoining; *Spencer Terrace*, and other edifices rose in succession under his creating influence. All these he furnished; and it is not to be wondered at that the immense expenditure, occasioned by his purchases of the ground, by his fitting up all these residences as comfortable abodes, that his purse became exhausted ere a correspondent return could be realised equal to the great capital employed. It appears by a manuscript account, that in 1795, the gross amount received from all these buildings was only 1919*l.* 5*s.* 6*d.* and in 1796, 1803*l.* 9*s.* 6*d*†.

Sir Richard Hotham, in consequence of the distance of Bersted Church from his new establishment, attached a very handsome chapel to his residence, thence called Chapel-House, for his distinguished visitors; but in this he was opposed by his friend, the vicar; and all the influence and interest which the founder of Bognor exerted with his accustomed energy and assiduity in higher quarters, failed to obtain its consecration. This

* Now the property of   Nixon, Esq.

† In the first mentioned year the following distinguished personages were at Bognor:

Earl Macclesfield	Lord Pembroke	Lady Uxbridge
Earl Spencer	Lady Pembroke	Hon. Miss Byng
Duke of Devonshire	Lord Dunwar	Sir Edward Leslie
The Speaker	Duchess of Rutland	Mr. Lewis, M. P.
Lord Lucan	Lady Jane Halliday	Mr. Sheridan, M .P.
Lord R. Fitzgerald	Lady Grantham	Mr. Tierney, M. P.
Hon. Mr. Gage	Lady Rushout	

and many others of rank and quality.

And in 1796 the following, with many other fashionables: His R. H. The Prince, Lady E. Drummond, Lady A. Thorpe, Earl of Jersey, Countess of Dunmore, Sir John Webb, Dowager Lady Albemarle, Lady S. Thorpe.

was for several years a source of great mortification and vexation. At length however his patience and perseverance were gratified and all difficulties were overcome. Several popular ministers performed divine service to numerous and fashionable auditors, and at Sir Richard's death the officiating chaplain was the Rev. Seth Thompson.

No pains were left untried to make Bognor a popular abode. The object of the founder was to render it a select and quiet abode, distinguished from all other places of a similar description; and that it met with great encouragement amongst the *haut ton*, the list of distinguished personages named in the notes subjoined abundantly evince. It is a natural propensity of the human mind to deceive itself, and to be flattered with illusory hopes and expectations, when a favorite project seizes upon the attention. Resolutely bent on the pursuit of a particular object, and deeply impressed with the certainty of its ultimate success, some men of strong understandings will never abandon a favorite project till ruin overtake them, or death stop their career, whilst men of weak minds, acting upon prudential motives, fearful of consequences, and easily turned aside from their purpose by temporary difficulties, recede in time, and save themselves and families from the impending danger.

It must have been obvious to a steady calculator that the income derivable from furnished lodgings upon so large a scale, where the proprietors must be necessarily subject to numerous defalcations through the waste and carelessness of servants,—the inattention of agents—the immense deduction for all sorts of taxes—the constant deterioration in the value of household furniture by wear and tear,—and the necessity to supply others to keep up the credit of the establishment, could never have secured returns for the large capital employed; and this appalling fact, as the result unfolded itself, added to the exhaustion of his large fortune, and the accumulation of pressing demands, prayed deeply on the founder's mind as he advanced in years. Still he exerted himself with ceaseless activity to realise his views; and, as he possessed a mind not easily overcome by disappointments, he went on adopting every plan that could forward and complete his views, with apparent cheerfulness and spirit—still making, as he had always done, his abode the seat of hospitality and good cheer. In the latter part of his life, he was engaged in a very expensive law suit respecting the distribution of some prize-money to which he laid claim on account of one of his vessels being in sight at the time of a very valuable capture from the enemy. From the successful termination of this suit, he expected to replenish his purse, and to be enabled to continue and complete his plans. At length, however, the law's delay terminated in an unfavourable issue to his fondest hopes; and he not only lost all participation in the expected prize, but was subject to the payment of a large sum for costs. This circumstance, and increasing cares, added to the weight of years, at length broke in upon his health; and at the age of 76, (possessed a few years before of florid health and an energetic mind,) he bade adieu to all the concerns of life and sought repose in a better and a happier world. A plain slab of black marble near to the entrance of Bersted Church records his death, as happening on the 14th. of March, 1799; but his virtues will long live in the recollection of his contemporaries, until *they* are summoned to the same fate*.

After Sir Richard Hotham's decease, his property was all sold to pay off incumbrances; and, out of the large fortune he possessed when he embarked in his great undertaking, the net amount very little exceeded 12000*l*.

In thus rapidly sketching the origin of Bognor, we had forgotten to state that as there was no Inn or Public House in the place, except an old one with a thatched roof, called "The Fox," situate at some little distance from the sea, Sir Richard Hotham purchased the same, and enlarged it into a very handsome Hotel, with a suite of rooms adapted for the accommodation of visitors until they could settle themselves into comfortable houses or lodgings, or for their temporary abode, if they preferred an hotel to private apartments. Detached from, or very near to, the hotel, was a very handsome reading room, within a few yards of the sea, commanding views bounded only by the horizon, which formed a very agreeable lounge,

---

* Dr. Davis, speaking of Sir Richard's grave, has very beautifully applied to him the following simple and elegant lines of Florian:

"Dans cette demeure tranquille
Repose notre bon ami;
Il vecut toujours à la ville
Mais son cœur fut toujours Ici."

During this year the following distinguished persons were visitors at Bognor.

Duchess of Bolton	Countess Dowager Albemarle	Hon. Clotworthy Rowley
Marquis of Lansdowne	Lord Harburton	Mrs. Barwell
Count Starhemberg	Lady Nugent	Sir John Orde
Lady Clifford	Lady Musgrove	
Lady Dalling		

and many other persons trés distinguès.

and where concerts and balls in Bognor's happiest hours were frequently celebrated. A very extensive stabling and covered way for carriages were also erected at the back part of the hotel, and the whole was considered at that period as one of the most convenient and extensive establishments of the kind in Sussex. After continuing in the hands of several successive tenants with various success, and mainly contributing to the prosperity of the town, by affording accommodations to the general visitors, and to the inhabitants at large, the latter had the mortification in the month of June, 1826, to see this extensive edifice with all its appendages, accidentally destroyed by fire. By this calamity, and by the want of another regular establishment of a similar description, the inhabitants and visitors of lodging-houses sustained a severe loss. The fire reached to Rock Buildings; and fears were once entertained that the whole of that row of lodging houses would be destroyed. It extended still more westward and burnt down sixteen cottages; but by the exertions of the inhabitants, and the arrival of engines from Chichester, the flames were at length got under; not however without rendering several poor and industrious families houseless, for whose relief a liberal subscription was raised.

It should be added that the founder of Bognor was extremely desirous of immortalizing his name, by changing that of Bognor into "HOTHAMTON," by which appellation it was, from courtesy towards him, distinguished during his life; but soon afterwards, to the regret of many persons, it resumed its former name.

A very handsome and capacious hotel called *The Norfolk Hotel*, has been erected near the scite of that which was burnt down, and is beautifully situated. It is occupied by Mr. Lock, who has a choice cellar of wines and liqueurs.

CHAPTER IV.

Further description of Bognor.

BOGNOR is situate about seven miles from Chichester and Littlehampton; from Arundel ten and three quarters; from Worthing seventeen; from Brighton twenty eight; and from London about sixty four.

The coast to the east of Bognor winds gently to the left; and then, taking another turn, advances into the sea, terminating at the point wherein is now situated the flourishing town of Worthing. After this the land is again encroached upon by the ocean, which, in its turn, is once more advanced upon by the territory around Brighton. Owing to the ingress of the sea, between the point where Worthing rises to the view and the hills of Brighton, the elevated country of the latter, has literally the appearance of a shore, entirely separated from the beholder at Bognor. The high land which we then discover at a distance, makes a finish to the landscape that is exceedingly interesting.

The plain on which Bognor is situated is open to the east, and therefore receives all the genial influence of the sun from the moment it appears above the horizon; but it is nevertheless infinitely less exposed to the influence of winds coming from that quarter of the heavens than Worthing.

The air of Bognor is remarkable for its mildness and salubrity. The invalid on visiting its shores soon finds an increase of appetite and a renovation of health. It is defended from the chilling blasts of the north by that immense chain of hills called the *South Downs*, which stretch themselves from Dover to Portsmouth, and which were probably connected in ancient times with those in the Isle of Wight, but separated therefrom by some great convulsion of nature. The mildness of its temperature is visible in the luxuriance of the trees and shrubs that grow near the shore, and the facility with which all sorts of native and many exotic plants are cultivated; whilst at Brighton, and some other parts of the coast, which are exposed to the impetuous blasts of the ocean, scarcely a tree is to be seen. At the very edge, indeed, of the ocean, at this place, and during several of the winter months, the elegant *Tamarisk** is seen to luxuriate and blossom in full perfection, and whilst the snow, during those months, lies embedded on the northern side of the hills, it is either not seen here, or soon dissolves away under the genial influence of the climate. *Bognor*, therefore, is peculiarly fitted for the residence of the invalid, being equally removed from the chilling influence of the northern, and the enervating warmth of the southern, winds. The sands decline gradually from the shore to the native bed of the ocean; and children may perambulate their smooth and elastic surface with perfect safety. The rides in the neighbourhood are not incumbered with turnpikes, a very

---

* Of the class pentandria and order of trigynia, and ranging under the 13th. order succulentæ. There are four species easily raised by cuttings.

material circumstance in the expenditure of those who keep horses and carriages; the roads are good, through a country highly cultivated; amid pleasant villages, where squalid poverty, or roofless and decayed cottages, are seldom seen. The independence and riches of the yeomanry are visible in their neat and well furnished farm-houses and extensive gardens and orchards; and their pleasant manners and superior understandings shew how rapid has been "the march of intellect" within these few years. The comforts and happiness, indeed, enjoyed by a British and affluent farmer, in modern times, remind us of the description of a rural life in the Augustan age as recorded by the Mantuan bard.

"Hic secura quies et nescia fallere vita
Dives opum variarum, hic latis otia fundis
Speluncæ, vivique lacus, hic frigide Tempe
Mugitusque boûm, mollesque sub arbore somni
Non absunt."

In calm reposing, with an honest life,
That shuns deceit and will not kindle strife;
With riches, and with home-bred plenty, blest,
And mild content his ever constant guest;
The rural king his cooling shade enjoys,
With running brooks far from the city's noise.
His lowing herds thro' the rich valley stray,
And sleep succeeds the labour of the day.

This feeling is more strongly excited in surveying the country round Bognor from any high eminence. From Dome House, for instance, the view is particularly gratifying, and offers a perfect panorama of beautiful scenery. The eye from this spot ranges over a vast extent of country. The Isle of Wight, rising majestically from the ocean, its blue hills stretching out to the west, till they are lost in the dim distance—the peninsula of Selsey underneath—the Portsdown hills—the beautiful and picturesque domain of the Duke of Richmond, Slindon, Dale Park, with their woods, forests, mansions, rich vales, cultivated grounds, churches, hamlets, farm-houses, and cottages dotted here and there, flocks and herds, all bespeaking a land flowing with milk and honey, and manifesting the bountiful gifts of providence to man. In surveying these how can we help exclaiming with the poet?

> England with all thy faults I love thee still
> My country! and whilst yet a nook is left
> Where English minds and manners can be found,
> Shall be constrained to love thee. Tho' thy clime
> Be fickle, and thy year most part deformed
> With dripping rains, or withered by a frost,
> I would not yet exchange thy sullen skies,
> And fields without a flower, for warmer France
> With all her vines, nor for Ausonia's groves
> Of golden fruitage, or her myrtle bowers!

The soil of Bognor is a rich loam, chiefly upon a reddish brick earth, of which bricks have lately been made in large quantities by the London Brick Company; then appears sand or gravel, and sometimes a white and marly and binding earth. Below this other argillaceous substances, of a black colour, (*a*) and of a sulphureous smell, abound; particularly below the shore where the sea flows, which by its action has carried away the upper stratum of the soil. In this clay is found imbedded the kidney rock, or clay nodules, used for making cement, which form themselves into hard substances by the deposition of the iron ore with which the coast abounds.

(*a*) I believe the London Clay.

Bognor Rocks extend into the sea in a curved direction, from east to west about two miles, and probably much more. Of late years they have supplied the builder with materials for the erection of houses and walls, to the great injury, in the estimation of many persons, of the proprietors of estates near the sea, whose encroachments on the land have lately been truly alarming. These rocks are composed of pyritical granite in separate masses, and visible only at low water.

From this general description of Bognor we proceed to other particulars.

Arran Lodge, is formed principally out of two houses which were erected by Sir Richard Hotham as forming the east wing of The Crescent. These have received very considerable additions and alterations by the late noble proprietor, and no expence has been spared in the erection of hot-houses, pineries, succession-houses, and conservatories. The hand of taste is visible in the laying out the grounds, walks, and shrubberries, which, altogether, form a perfect Elysium. The residence of the Earl and the large expenditure of an extensive establishment was of great advantage to the tradesmen and inhabitants. It is now the property and residence of Lord Geo. H. Lennox.

Dome House was the property of the late Charles Edward Wilsonn, Esq. who was also the proprietor of the two houses immediately adjoining. Sir Richard Hotham had fancied that His late Majesty Geo. III, might have been induced to reside a short time at this mansion, and therefore he laid out the rooms accordingly—and it is unquestionably one of the best houses in Bognor. The late lamented Princess Charlotte resided in

BOGNOR LODGE.

Dean & Munday, Lithographers, Threadneedle St.

[illegible] , and [illegible] man [illegible]

[illegible] It is [illegible] villa is [illegible] ting with the [illegible] to form [illegible]

[illegible] charities, [illegible] ing and edu[illegible] twenty [illegible]

Dome House, who, had Providence spared her life, would have been a great patroness to the town, her Royal Highness preferring Bognor to all other places of a similar description.

Bersted Lodge, formerly Chapel House.—This has undergone considerable improvements since it came into the possession of the late Mr. Smith, more particularly in turning the public road, and thereby enlarging the ground in front of the mansion. Additional lands have been purchased surrounding the house, a ferme orneé made, and the whole estatė rendered fit for the residence and occupation of a person of fortune*.

Bognor Lodge was built and occupied by the late Sir Richard Hotham, before he erected Chapel-House, and was lately purchased by the Earl of Arran with all the lands attached to it from Sir John Harington, Bart. It is now the property of Mr. Pearson.

Sudley Lodge is the property of Wm. Groom, Esq. whose taste has been eminently displayed in the erection and fitting up of this very neat and handsome villa and its appendages, and in the disposal of and laying out the grounds attached thereto. It is occupied by P. P. Fitzpatrick Esq.

This villa is understood to be part of a plan originating with the Earl of Arran, the object of which is to form a series of villas on the grounds lately Sir John Harington's, so as to render Bognor a place of resort unique in its kind, and to be distinguished from all others on the coast,

* It ought to be recorded to the honour of the lady who is now the proprietress of this estate, that independent of numerous private charities, she has long established a school for the clothing and education of twenty poor girls.

where houses are in general congregated together like trading towns, and the free circulation of air impeded by masses of buildings crowded together in one small spot. It is sincerely to be hoped that this excellent plan will be followed up.

Sudley Cottage adjoins Sudley Lodge, and was erected by Mrs. Esdaile, having been removed from Aldwick in consequence of the encroachment of the sea. It is now the property and residence of Christopher Teesdale, Esq.

Sudley Terrace.—These very handsome houses situate near the New Inn, have lately been erected by Mr. Wonham, Junior, for lodging houses, and are now fitted up with every convenience for visitors.

Sudley Stables, lately erected, and the coach-houses connected with them are formed upon a plan superior to almost any modern buildings of the same description, and are a great acquisition to the place, as doing away with complaints which had long existed of the want of such an establishment.

The Royal Clarence Hotel.—This costly and superb structure, and the Baths adjoining were erected at a great expence for the accommodation of the public, and are almost unequalled on the coast. The plan of these and of the adjoining buildings designated "The New Crescent," is the production of Mr. Beazley.

The New Inn Hotel, near to the high road, is a good house of entertainment, and well conducted by the worthy host, Mr. Hart, who has some excellent wines, &c.

York House is a bold and prominent building, extremely well situated for the temporary residence of a family of distinction, and combines every desirable comfort both in its fitting up and in the furniture contained in it. It is now converted into an Hotel, well adapted for the reception of visitors.

East Row and Hothampton Row are separate suites of good lodging houses, erected by Sir Richard Hotham. They are of a good elevation, have a carriage drive and plantation in front, and, facing the sea with an intervening meadow, possess peculiar advantages.

The Jubilee School. This is an excellent institution, supported by voluntary contributions, for the education of fifty poor girls. It was established on his late Majesty Geo. the 3rd. reaching the 50th anniversary of his reign, through the exertions of Mrs. Wilsonn, aided by her Late Royal Highness the Princess Charlotte.

St. John's Chapel was erected on speculation by Mr. Wonham, and has been since consecrated. Divine service is regularly performed twice every Sunday. The stipend of the Chaplain and the repairs of the building are paid out of the rent of the pews, which are let either by the year or for any other definite period. The place is well chosen for the occasion, and is a great accommodation to the visitors and inhabitants on account of the distance of the parish church, and its inadequacy to accommodate the increasing population.

The Market House is near to the last mentioned building. This was erected on the speculation of a private individual, and an act of parliament, after much opposition from the inhabitants, obtained, as well for the regulation of the market as for the establishment of a police for the town, and for its internal improvement. Two other acts of parliament have been passed for the improvement of the town, for establishing a police, for making roads, and for lighting and watching the same. Commissioners are appointed who meet often for the dispatch of business. The government of the market and the regulation of the dues and the duties on coal, &c. are under the control and management of these gentlemen.

The Library and Billiard Room. These are under the management of the Misses Binstead. The library contains a collection of the best modern publications, and the daily and provincial papers and several reviews are taken in and placed on the reading table for the use of the subscribers—nor can there be a better or more elegant assortment of *bijouterie*, bronze and china ornaments, stationary and all other *desiderata* of this description, than are to be found at this fashionable resort. There is also another library, kept by H. Hounsom, successor to Mr. Knapton, who is the postmaster, and who also deals very extensively in articles of jewellery, rich china and other ornaments.

The Steyne is a place peculiarly fitted for lodging houses, being open to the sea, and having in the centre a promenade for the occupiers inclosed from the roads on each side. Some excellent lodging houses are to be met with on this spot, which is considered the pleasantest in the place. The vacant pieces of ground, however, on each side deteriorates in some measure from the present value of the buildings there, but when these are built on, with handsome elevations, the Steyne must be the favorite resort of visitors. Some baths of a very superior description have been erected here at Bath-house, which of itself is formed on a plan worthy of imitation, and is let as a lodging house.

The Norfolk Hotel is a splendid establishment near the sea, lately erected by A. L. Sarel, Esq. and is kept by Mr. Lock. Here is every convenience for families upon a large scale. The situation is peculiarly well chosen, and the choicest wines are sure to be obtained.

The Claremont Hotel, near the Steyne, has been erected since the destruction of the Hotel by fire. It is a most desirable residence for small families during the season, and is much resorted to on account of its peculiar comforts, and the neatness and regularity with which the whole establishment is conducted.

Rock Buildings.—These houses, the property of Mr. Wonham, are, from their immediate contiguity to the sea, and the comforts and accommodation they combine, generally the first let during the bathing season. They are situate westward of the late hotel, have a complete view of the ocean, the peninsula of Selsey and the Isle of Wight, and form a handsome object on the coast.

Butchers' Meat.—No place in England can boast of better meat, or of neater or more cleanly butchers' shops than Bognor. The true South Down mutton is to be had in the greatest perfection, and at the usual market price.

Fish, Lobsters, Prawns &c.—For want of a regular establishment, Bognor is not supplied with fish so well or at such cheap prices as it ought to be. The lobsters, prawns, and shrimps are of a very superior flavor*.

* "Sussex does boast of several fish, as namely, a Selsey cockle, a Chichester lobster, an Arundel mullet, and an Amberley Trout." *Isaac Walton.*

The "Chichester Lobster" means those brought to the Chi-

Fresh Water.—Of this, complaint has seldom been made. It is in general soft, pure and good—and there is a remarkable well containing some of the purest in England, at the Mews near Spencer Terrace, which was formerly in great repute among the inhabitants.

Springs, &c.—It has been asserted that there are Chalybeate springs in this neighbourhood, but they have not hitherto been discovered, probably because not sought after. It is certain that the shore produces iron or copperas ore, containing a mixture of cobalt and sulphur, large quantities of which are scattered along the shore, and were formerly picked up by the poor and sold to a tanner at Stockbridge near Chichester, who paid a rent to the Lord of the Manor for the same, and to the poor for collecting, threepence per bushel.

Plants, &c.—The sea spinach (*spinica maritima*) is gathered on the shore and at Felpham and Aldwick, and capable of being transplanted to the gardens, but it is not so good as the common garden spinach.

The golden samphire (*inula crithmoides*) sold by some persons as equal to the Isle of Wight Samphire (*crithmum maritimum*) but of very different quality. The fallacy may be detected by tasting. In the genuine samphire the stalks are *succulent*, the leaves *pinnate*, (winged or feather formed) of three or five divisions, each having as many small thick lance shaped leaves. Both these and the stalk have a pungent taste. In the

---

chester market from Bognor and Selsey. Arundel is still famous for Mullets, and Amberley for trout and eels: and another species of mullet is caught off Bognor and frequently exposed for sale.

false species, the stalk on the contrary is roundish, jointed, and tasteless, with a tough string running through the middle of it, instead of the flat leaf of the *crishmum maritimum*.

Neottia Spiralis, or Lady's Tapes, on the lawn at Chapel House, supposed to have been brought thither by accident, as it is not elsewhere in the neighbourhood.

Cheledoniium Glaucium, Yellow Horned Poppy, *Geranium Maritimum*, Sea Crane's Bill, both found at Bognor and Aldwick.

Antirhinum cymbalaria, Ivy leaved toad flax, on the walls of Bognor and Felpham.

Frankinia pulverulenta, Powdery sea heath, on the coast between Bognor and Brighton.

Erodium maritimum, Sea heron's bill, on the shore near Bognor Rocks.

Fucus ruscifolius, Rushy sea weed at Bognor.

Ulva compressa, Flat Laver, at Bognor Rocks.

Conserva rupestris, Rock conserva, or sea beard, on the rocks.

After heavy storms some curious aquatic plants are driven ashore, supposed to come from the Isle of Wight, of which very handsome collections are formed. The most distinguished kind is the *fucus albidus*, or white sea weed, but there are many others that will afford amusement to those who make this part of the vegetable world their study.

Pebbles, *Agates*, *&c.*—Of these many beautiful specimens are picked up on the shore, and necklaces, bracelets, brooches, and other personal ornaments made, by regular pebble polishers, settled at Bognor, whose collections are well worthy of inspection, and whose moderate prices deserve encouragement.

Fossils.—The fossiologist will not receive much gratification at Bognor. Still, there are now and then a few scarce specimens of fossil remains of shells and fish to be met with, which are procured from those who are employed to separate the rocks from their native beds, and to break and shape them for pavement or building. In these are sometimes found *turbinated* and bivalved shells of various species, either now altogether unknown, or found only in tropical climates.

RIDES, WALKS, &c.

1. To *Chichester*. 2. To *Goodwood* and *Cairney's Seat* there. 3. To *Arundel* and the *Castle*. 4. To *Littlehampton*. 5. To *Slindon*, the seat of the Countess of Newburgh. 6. A short ride nearer home is to *Aldwick* and *Pagham*.

7. Excursions are made by water to Selsey, the Owers Lights, to Littlehampton and Worthing—and sometimes to the Isle of Wight.

8. A very pleasant, though short ramble, may be made from Bognor through the fields to Bersted, and thence to Felpham—but the stiles which it becomes necessary to cross on this occasion, are a great impediment to its enjoyment by the ladies.

The views in the fields near Felpham on this route are of a particularly pleasing character. In front you see the tower of the church and the village, partially hid by trees, on the right the buildings of the Crescent, Arran Lodge, &c. and on the left, a rich inland country, dotted with farm houses and cottages, bounded by the downs, the intervening space pleasing the eye with its rich and variegated hues. Accustomed to behold the bright and sparkling waters of the ocean, it is a great relief to view the green meadows, the varied foliage of the wide spreading trees, that adorn this part of the country, the cattle silently grazing in the pastures, the waving corn ripening for the sickle, and the quiet and picturesque scenes of this beautiful spot.

BOGNOR CHARITABLE INSTITUTIONS,

extending to North and South Bersted, Shripney, Lidsey, Aldwick, &c.

Inquiries being often made by strangers resorting to Bognor, as to the number and nature of its Charitable Institutions, the following short statement of them is made public.

JUBILEE (NATIONAL) SCHOOL FOR GIRLS;

Instituted October 25th. 1809, under the Patronage of her late Royal Highness, the Princess Charlotte of Wales, to commemorate her Venerable Grandfather's entering into the 50th. year of his reign.

NATIONAL SCHOOL FOR BOYS, AT BERSTED;

INFANT'S SCHOOL, FOR CHILDREN FROM 18 MONTHS TO 7 YEARS OF AGE.

SUNDAY SCHOOLS FOR BOYS AND GIRLS;

AND SUNDAY EVENING SCHOOLS FOR ADULTS.

Besides the above Public Parish Schools, there is an Institution for Twenty Poor Girls, who are clothed and instructed in reading, sewing, and other useful works of Housewifery, at the sole charge of Mrs. Smith, of Bersted Lodge, Bognor.

DISTRICT VISITING SOCIETY.

To promote a general systematic visiting of the Poor in Bognor, with a view of improving their temporal and spiritual condition, to prevent also the impositions of vagrant petitioners, and the evils of indiscriminate charity. Printed Tickets for distribution to the poor of Coals, Soup, and Bread, &c. at reduced prices may be obtained at the Parsonage, also for the same purpose, Bibles, Testaments, and Prayer Books, at very small cost.

LYING-IN CHARITY.

The object of this Institution is to purchase Linen, &c. &c. for the use of poor married women, during their Confinement, and to allow each woman 5s. in money.

CLOTHING FUND.

For encouraging the industrious by small weekly deposits to furnish themselves with Clothing at the end of the year.

FEMALE FRIENDLY AND MUTUAL ASSURANCE SOCIETY;

For the maintenance and relief of the Contributors thereto, by a system of mutual assurance and friendly support, in Infancy, Sickness, Infirmity, and Old Age.

BRANCH SAVINGS BANKS;

To enable Labourers, Servants, and all industrious Persons, to make deposits in the "Chichester Savings Bank."

FIELD GARDENS;

Granting the Labourer at a fair rent, such an allotment of land, as he can cultivate without neglecting his ordinary employment. During the winter months, Tenants under 19 years of age, are required to attend an Evening School.

A DISTRICT COMMITTEE OF THE SOCIETY FOR THE PROPAGATION OF THE GOSPEL IN FOREIGN PARTS.

A LENDING LIBRARY,

For the use of the Poor, gratis; at the Jubilee School, Bognor, and at the National Boys' School, Bersted.

*** The above sketch, it is hoped, will meet the views of such Visitors as may wish, in return for health restored, to leave a blessing behind them, upon some one or more of the Charitable Institutions of Bognor. The Reports of the different Institutions may be had, and Subscriptions for the same are received at the Parsonage, Bognor, and at the Vicarage, Bersted.

CHAPTER V.

FURTHER DESCRIPTION OF

SOUTH-BERSTED.

General improvements—ancient name—the church—population, &c.

THE spirit of improvement manifested throughout Bognor, and the patronage it experienced, naturally extended itself to the adjoining districts—and those of South and North-Bersted, as lying within the immediate proximity, soon felt its effects. From having been a dull dirty village, South-Bersted is now become lively and clean. The old Vicarage House has been taken down, and a handsome structure, more fitted for the abode of a gentleman, of simple gothic architecture, has heen erected instead. Farm houses and cottages have been improved; a School for the tuition of boys according to the system of Dr. Bell, has been established; and the whole place bearing evident marks of a progressive state of amelioration and amendment, which are chiefly owing to the efforts of the present worthy vicar. The plantations and grounds attached to the Vicarage House are laid out with singular good taste and beauty. The scenery from the vicarage garden is eminently calculated to impress on the mind a tranquillity and repose peculiarly fitted for that which should characterize a minister of the gospel, destined to perform the sacred functions of his office in the church opposite thereto.

The name was anciently spelt *Berghestede*, and had sometimes the appellation of Berghamstede, otherwise Berghestede South. Stephen de Berghestede was consecrated Bishop of Chichester in 1262, and was a native of this place. He is stated to have been a man of great innocence and simplicity, and to have been afflicted with blindness for many years.

The church has nothing to recommend it to the notice of the antiquary. It has a nave and two aisles, with a small vestry room: and the whole of the interior is particularly neat. It was completely pewed a century ago, at the expence of Thomas Grey, of Shripney. The gallery was erected at the expence of Sir Richard Hotham, under the authority of a Faculty from the Archbishop's Court of peculiars at Chichester.

Monuments, &c. in the Church.

ANCIENT INSCRIPTION ON THE LEFT SIDE OF THE CHANCEL.

HEĀRE LYETH THE BODY OF
IOHN HĀMĀN WHO DECEĀSED
THE 26 DĀY OF MĀRCH IN THE
YEĀRE OF OVR LORD
1681.

On a white marble slab in the interior of the church, on the south side of the chancel, is a very pleasing memorial on the death of Frances Jane, daughter of Richard Hasler, Esq. and of Martha, his wife. It represents a female rising from the tomb, and flying towards heaven; near which is a lily snapped asunder from its root. The monument has the following inscription.

FRANCES! thy fleeting life is o'er,
  To twice seven years confined;
Yet still thy little span was more
  Than that of half mankind.
This tablet, pure as parents' love,
  Thy parents' grief must show,
And tell how brief best blessings prove,
  How transient joy and woe.

Also one to the memory of Thomas Newland Hasler, born November 30, 1808, died November 30, 1813.

Late sent from heaven, and bound to earth
  By nature's weakest ties:
Unstained he sought a second birth,
  In heaven again to rise;
His sister cherub led the way,
  And beckoning from on high,
Drew from the bonds of beauteous clay
  The cherub to the sky.

And another to the memory of Martha Hasler, born February 1st 1803, died October 7th. 1815.

Dear sainted child, whom we to God resign,
In tears, obedient to decrees divine,
Angelic Martha! if from realms of rest,
Thou view thy parents, by thy loss opprest,
While we contemplate, in this world of strife,
Thy Christian virtues, and thy blameless life,
Aid us, as here thy path to Heaven we trace,
To gain, as thou hast gained, thy Saviour's grace.

In the Churchyard, between the tomb of Henry Pollington and the foot stone near the yew tree, is a very ancient grave stone of a coffin shape, with the figure of the cross having seven radii, or points. It was recently taken from a grave close to the Yew. This cross was borne by the knights of the order of St. John of Jerusalem, and their officers, some of whom were settled in the manor of that name at Rumboldswyke, near Chichester. And there is another stone of a similar description in the south side of the outer wall of the chancel in the same churchyard.

The Benefice is vicarial, within the Deanery of Pagham. The Archbishop is the patron. The Rev. Edward Eedle is the present vicar.

The soil of the parish consists of a rich strong loam, requiring little manure, except marle, for the produce of wheat of superior quality, which is as abundant as any district in the county, except Pagham, which is still more fertile.

The land in tillage in the whole parish is estimated at 1260 statute acres, with a small proportion of pasture. The form is nearly square, extending two miles and a half by two miles.

The Manors are *North-Bersted*, *South-Bersted*, and *Shripney*. Of the first a grant was made by the crown to William Lord Craven, in 1644. In 1785 his descendant sold it to Richard Barwell, Esq. and by his trustees it was sold in 1812 to William Brereton, Esq. whose devisees now possess it.—South-Bersted belongs to William Potts, Esq.—Shripney, or Shrympney, or Sharpinè, is held together with North-Bersted.

The great tythes of the parish were formerly held by the Gooch family, by lease from the Dean and Chapter of Canterbury, and in 1811 were purchased by John Hasler, Esq. and are now the property of his nephew, Richard Hasler, Esq.

The population, including Bognor, in 1821 was 1851, and according to the last census, in 1831—2190.

CHAPTER VI.

FELPHAM.

IMMEDIATELY adjoining to the parish last described, is the very pleasant village of Felpham.

Felpham, or as it was sometimes anciently written, "Felgeham," was a village or manor as early as the reign of King Alfred, by whom, with other parishes and manors, it was bequeathed to his nephew Osferth.

The manor and lands at Felpham are mentioned in Domesday Book under the name of Falcheham, as belonging to the Abbot of St. Edward's, and under the Saxon government, as valued at ten pounds per annum, but at the time of the compilation of Domesday estimated at twenty. In the same record a church is mentioned to have been then subsisting in this parish.

The parish is part of the Rape of Arundel, and within the Hundred of Avisford. In the 23rd Edward I. free warren in the manor was granted to the Abbess de Felgeham, and in the 2nd Edward II. it appears that the Abbess of Shaftsbury paid a fine to the king for Felgeham, so that the manor must have passed from the Abbey of Felpham to the latter monastary.

There is reason to believe that the ancient mansion in Felpham, belonging to the Rev. Archdeacon Webber, and held with the great tithes under the Dean and Chapter of Chichester, was the scite of the ancient monastery, on the dissolution of which it was conferred by Henry VIII. on that body. The rectory is a sinecure.—

The vicarage was endowed in 1345. The Rev. John Beed is the present vicar.

The mansion house before mentioned was occupied for several years by the late Dr. Cycil Jackson, who resigned the Deanery of Christ Church; and that learned man spent his last days in this retired spot.

To his memory a plain tomb is erected in the church yard, simply recording the period of his death, with the following inscription:

> "Enter not into judgment with thy servant O Lord, for in thy sight can no man living be justified."

This venerable man and excellent scholar, on whose head mitres were ready to be showered down, had he pleased to accept them, was tutor to Geo. IV. and from him, whilst Prince Regent, in the last moments of existence, he received a visit at Felpham. The prince taking him by the hand, affectionately addressed him. The latter, then almost in the arms of death, turned his eye on his Sovereign, but knew him not; the lamp of life was rapidly waning, and soon after went out. The prince turned aside and wept; and recalling to his mind the scenes and impression of days gone by, he silently left the chamber of death, deeply regretting that his interview with the mentor of his youth had been so long procrastinated.

The Church retains the ancient open seats of oak with some pews, but it has not the cleanly and neat appearance of South-Bersted. It has a nave and two aisles, with a large chancel, which has been altered from its original style by repairs. The tower is a square and solid structure, and is characteristic of the architecture prevalent at the age of Henry VII. Some parts of the church, the remains probably of the old, shew greater antiquity.

In the church is a font of Saxon or Norman origin, and of a size sufficiently large for the total immersion of the infant. Near the chancel, and within the communion railing, are some Roman or Norman tiles, which denote the antiquity of the church, or at least of that on the scite of which the present one is built. A black marble slab within the rails, covers the mortal remains of some unknown, whose memory no inscription has handed down to us. In the tower is a ring of four bells.—The first has on it "Sic nomen domini benedictum." The second is of the date of 1627. The third of the date of 1589. The fourth "Anno domini 1600, Hy. Tarvel."

Monumental inscriptions. "*Roger Sparkes, ob.*" 1679. (This respectable family, in various branches, still reside at Felpham and in the neighbourhood.)

On a marble tablet near the chancel is an inscription to the memory of Robert Steele, Esq. Recorder of Chichester, (father of the late Thómas and Right Hon. Robert Steele, both of whom died without issue). "*He lived a pattern worthy of imitation as a friend a father and a husband, and for many years fulfilled the public duties of a magistrate with integrity and justice. He died universally beloved and universally lamented,* Sept. 29, 1775, Ætat 53." In a vault adjoining lie interred the remains of his son Robert, also Recorder of Chichester, with merely the initials of his name, R. S. on a small marble stone let into the floor. He was a worthy man and of the most honorable cast of character. He died A. D. 1817.

In the same vault repose the ashes of the late poet Hayley. They had been school-fellows. To his memory has lately been erected a plain marble monument, on which is the following inscription from the pen of Mrs. Opie, with whom, and with her deceased husband he was acquainted.

HAYLEY! beloved friend! tho' round thy head
The muse's wreath its grateful foliage spread;
Tho' Fame was long thy talents' rich reward,
And Fashion smiled upon SERENA'S bard;
Tho' thou wast form'd in polished courts to shine,
And learning's stores and playful wit was thine;
Tho' COWPER'S self thy tuneful strains approved,
And praised the poet while the man he loved,
Cowper, who lives in thy recording page,
To interest, charm, and teach the future age;—
Oh! not on these alone thy honours rest,
But, that thy name pale want and misery blest!
That, such thy glowing zeal for all mankind,
So vast thy charity so unconfined,
Thy hand had spread a scene of blessing round,
If ample wealth thy ardent hopes had crown'd—
That, whatsoe'er thy bounty could impart,
Was given to teach the mind, and cheer the heart;
Neglected talent's drooping head to raise,
And lead young genius on by generous praise.—
Yet, bard beloved! this higher meed be thine,
Faith in thy Saviour cheered thy life's decline,—

Nor by that God on whom thy hopes relied,
Was the sweet recompence of faith denied.—
He gave thee strength to smile 'midst torturing pain,
And even the slightest murmur still restrain;
He cheered with pious hope thy dying bed,
He, on thy soul the Christian's sunshine shed,
And crown'd, to prove his favor's best increase,
A life of kindness and a death of peace.

Mr. Hayley, as is well known, resided for the last years of his life at this his favorite spot, in a villa of his own formation. He amply deserved all the high eulogiums which the elegant pen of Mrs. Opie has here recorded. Of him it may be justly said that if he had only written the life of Cowper, whose friendship for this "bard of Arun," as he was once called is well known, he would have been immortal.

His house stands nearly in the centre of the village, and was erected about the year 1800 for an occasional marine retreat; but was entirely occupied by him after the sale of his more extensive villa of Eartham to the Right Hon. W. Huskisson, with whom he was then in terms of equal intimacy. It is surrounded by a garden judiciously laid out, and has an extensive covered way for riding on horseback, of which the proprietor very frequently availed himself. His library was of the choicest kind, containing the most celebrated classics of the finest editions, and the best works in most of the modern European languages, in which Mr. Hayley was conversant, and which he studied with intense and weariless application. Many of these he had purchased in his travels on the Continent. His rooms, particularly his library, where he chiefly lived, were fitted up with singular taste, and adorned with busts, statues and pictures. Some of the portraits were the testamentary bequest of

Romney, whose Biography by Hayley is well known, and who was a frequent visitor both at Eartham and Felpham.—These portraits were, 1. Gibbon, sitting and as in conversation, in oil, a most striking likeness. 2. Cowper, head in crayon. 3. Mrs. Charlotte Smith, ditto. 4. Anna Seward, ditto. 5. Madame Genlis. 6. Emma Lyon, otherwise Hart, the celebrated but unfortunate Lady Hamilton, in several heads, and represented as Sensibility, Cassandra, Andromache, &c. 7. An admirable portrait of the Bard himself when young.

The house at Felpham was surmounted with a terrace commanding most extensive views. From hence the poet could cast his eye over the "world of waters blue and wide," and catch the last departing rays of the sun as it sunk below the horizon, and threw its golden gleams on the hemisphere it was about to quit; could listen to the hoarse murmurs of the ocean, rolling as it were at his feet, as its billows lashed the resounding shore,—interrupted only by the minstrels of the grove, or the busy hum of the little village below; and, turning northward, watch the fading landscape of his once loved Eartham, whose picturesque heights he had adorned and improved, whose trees he had planted, and whose walks he had laid out with all that singular felicity which marks the man of taste, who loves to revel in nature's choicest works, and which eminently distinguished this celebrated man. Still as his eye rolled over the sloping and verdant sides of his former abode, where he had cultivated the favor of the muses, and whence he had sent his "Triumphs of Temper" to the world,—an abode he had inherited from his father, whose memory he dearly cherished—he must have frequently heaved a sigh of regret that that fairy spot was no longer his, and that imperious fate had wrested it from him. But he was a man never given to complaint, and was so cheerfully and happily disposed, that he did not appear even to his most intimate friends to lament the loss; but found, in this sylvan and sequestered spot, amid his books and a very limited circle of friends, that enviable tranquillity which philosophic minds can only feel.

Scriptorum chorus omnis amat nemus et fugit urbes.
Hor. Ep.

The population of Felpham in 1821 was 581, and in 1831, 588.

CHAPTER VII.

MIDDLETON.

Contents of the parish in acres—Mentioned in Domesday—Sea encroachments—History of the manor—Elmer manor—The church—Views near it—Charlotte Smith's Sonnet.

From Felpham we proceed to the little village of Middleton. This parish now contains only about 300 statute acres, of which 40 or 50 are pasture and 11 wood. It appears however to have been formerly of sufficient consequence and value to have a place in Domesday Book, and is there stated to consist of a manor, lands in demesne, a church, &c. amounting in the whole to five hides and two virgates of land, and as part of the immense territories of Roger de Montgomery, Earl of Arundel, on whom, as chiefly contributing to the success obtained in the great Battle of Hastings, the Conqueror bestowed such ample domains.

For many years past the sea has been increasing on this parish, and has devastated and swallowed up a large portion of its rich and fair domain—Within a very short period of writing the first edition of this work, a cottage on the brink of the ocean, which once stood at an apparently safe distance from the shore, has been demolished. The walls of the church, now partly down, are washed by the tide, which has not spared the sacred depositaries of the dead, "whose bones have whitened in the frequent wave."

Elmer. To the east of Middleton, and in part of the same parish, is Elmer, which comprises about 150 acres. William De Elmere in the reign of Henry III. held half a knight's fee of the honour of Arundel.

Elmer is an exempted manor, and was originally held in demesne by the Earls of Arundel. Early in the last century it became the property of the family of Powys, and having been sold by the late Lord Lifford, has descended to Mr. Thomas Palmer the present proprietor.

The Benefice of Middleton is a Rectory in the Deanry of Arundel, and in the presentation of the Crown. The value has been gradually diminishing by means of the encroachments of the sea. There were formerly 24 acres belonging to the glebe. These in 1724 were reduced to 14, and are now not five. The manse is destroyed, and the Rector has a moiety only of the tithes of corn in Elmer. The present incumbent is the Rev. John Beed.

The Church, which stands on the brink of the ocean, was once much larger that it now is. This is sufficiently apparent by the Saxon arches which form the south side of the exterior, and which once enclosed the south aisle of the interior. In the body of the church are various coffin-shaped slabs of Sussex marble of great antiquity, and there are three antique carved oak chairs or seats, formerly placed in the chancel, which are fast yielding to the ravages of time, proving the truth of the adage, "*Tempus edax rerum.*" It is understood that the remains of the church are about to be removed to another part of the parish.

The celebrated Charlotte Smith, who was an acquaintance and visitor of Mr. Hayley's, frequently wandered near this spot. She was probably there, either in fancy or in reality, when the wild waves burst over the land, and threatened destruction to the yielding shore—and then with that facility with which genius catches the images before it, or in its mind's eye, and portrays them on its literary canvas, she sketched the following lines :

"Press'd by the moon, mute arbitress of tides,
   Whilst the loud equinox its power combines,
   The sea no more its swelling surf confines,
But o'er the shrinking land sublimely rides!

The wild blast rising from the western cave,
   Drives the huge billows from their heaving bed,
   Tears from their grassy tombs the village dead,
And breaks the silent Sabbath of the Grave.

With shells and sea-weed mingled on the shore,
   Lo! their bones whiten in the frequent wave,
   But vain to them the winds and waters rave,
They hear the warring elements no more:
   Whilst I am doom'd, by life's long storm oppress'd,
   To gaze with envy on their gloomy rest!"

The population of this small parish in 1821 was 44 and in 1831, 43.

Having thus conducted the reader to the two parishes immediately adjoining to Bognor on the east, we will now direct our attention westward, and give some useful information concerning the several parishes of Pagham and Selsey, first paying our respects to Aldwick, a tithing of the former parish, as lying contiguous to Bognor.

CHAPTER VIII.

ALDWICK.

The name is derived from the Saxon *eald*, old, and *vic*, a village. The place gives the name of the Hundred to the district, but that for some reason or other was changed from Pagham, by which alone when Domesday was compiled the hundred was named.

Aldwick being a constituent part of Pagham, is within the jurisdiction of the Archbishop of Canterbury. The village is situate about a mile west of Bognor, the tything commencing at a ditch near Nyewood Lane, which divides Aldwick from Bognor. It is accessible either along the shore, or by the new road made under the authority of an act of parliament.

The Manor of Aldwick on the death of Reginald Cardinal Pole, together with the Hundred Court of Pagham, fell into the hands of the Crown, and with other vast estates, was, in the 2nd. of Elizabeth, in consideration of 5214*l.* 9*s.* 7*d.* paid into the Exchequer, granted to Sir Richard Bakere, Knight, and Richard Sackville, Esq. who in the same year by virtue of a license of alienation, sold the manor and farm of Aldwick, (reserving the Hundred Court and all its profits and perquisites) to Thomas Sackville and John, afterwards Sir John, Dingley, of Wolverton in the Isle of Wight. Sir John Dingley subsequently became the purchaser of the other moiety of the said manor and farm, and made extensive grants of the demesne lands at Bognor, for long terms of years, reserving rents and feudal services to him and his heirs Lords of Aldwick. In the Dingley family the manor and farm continued till 1667, when they were purchased by John Combes, Esq. of Donnington, near Chichester, whose sister Mary becoming the wife of Mark Miller, an Alderman of Chichester, they passed in 1698 to his son Thomas, afterwards Sir Thomas, Miller, and was by his descendants sold to Sir Richard Hotham. On his death the manor was separated from the farm and was purchased by Colonel Scott, and subsequently by the editor of this work, and is now the property of the Devisees of William Brereton, Esq. deceased, who had purchased the manor farm under Sir Richard Hotham's will.

As to the Hundred Court, so reserved out of the sale to Thomas Sackville and John Dingley, which was also anciently attached to the see of Canterbury, it was ceded to Henry VIII by Archbishop Cranmer. In 1608 it was possessed by the Earl of Craven, and afterwards became the property of Richard Barwell, Esq. of Stanstead, and was by his Devisees sold to Mr. Brereton, whose Devisees have since purchased the manor late of

Mr. Dally; and his family therefore now possess Manor Farm and both the Manors of Aldwick, and the Hundred Court or Court Leet of Aldwick, attached and held therewith.

On the margin of the sea, and threatened by its inroads, stands in succession:

1. The residence late of Sir Simon Clarke, Bart. and now of Lady Clarke.

2 The picturesque and unique cottage of the late Sir Thomas Brooke Pechell, Bart. and now of Captain Sykes.

3. The villa built by the Countess of Newburgh, after an Italian model.

West Cottage, formerly belonging to, and occupied by, Mrs. Newnham, and lately by the Rev. Charles Baumgarten.

To which may be added on Aldwick Green, a handsome house lately belonging to Colonel Todd, and now to John Ord, Esq.

Sir Simon Clarke's house was erected by the late Alexander Williams, a respectable Wine Merchant at Chichester, and was for several years the property of General Stuart.

The pretty thatched cottage of Capt. Sykes cannot fail to attract admiration, from the simplicity of its structure and its rural appearance. The windows on the ground floor in the front are even with the lawn. Round the pillars which decorate the veranda are interwoven the rose, the jessamine, the honeysuckle, and other shrubs, which flourish in full luxuriance, though so near the sea; a plain evidence of the mildness and temperature of the air, and affording a delightful shade, which with the intervening verdure of the lawn, between the cottage and the ocean, form an agreeable relief to the glare of the sparkling and busy waters beneath.

Little more remains to be said of Aldwick. It is a quiet and sequestered spot, where the man of letters can retire and shut himself out from the world and all its noisy follies; where the mind may indulge itself in meditation; and Philosophy pursue her enlightened career without interruption—where the rippling ocean on the one side, and the calm scenery of this pretty village on the other, offer their charms to those who are capable of appreciating them; and to such, Aldwick will be ever loved and admired.

CHAPTER IX.

PAGHAM.

We have already stated that in that valuable and authentic document "Domesday," this place is called "Pagenham," and then gave the name to the hundred; no such name as Aldwick, by which the hundred is now called, being then known. Pagham was then held by the Archbishop of Canterbury in domain of the Crown. In the reign of King Edward it was rated at 50 hides(5000 acres) but contained much more. At the time of the compilation of the great national survey, of which Domesday is the record, it was said to be cleared for thirty four hides, and now, in fact, comprises about 4500 acres, 700 of which are pasture and 400 coppice.

The Hundred Court of Pagham or Pagenham (now called Aldwick Hundred Court), was given by Ceadwalla, King of the West Saxons to Wilfred, Bishop of Selsey, but soon transferred to the see of Canterbury*; and this village became the occasional residence of the Archbishops before they removed their palace to Slindon, on the site of which stands Slindon House, the residence of the Countess of Newburgh.

In the year 1208 Anselm was consecrated at Pagham, and in 1267 Richard Beleims, Bishop of London underwent the same ceremony at the same place†. Thomas á Becket was frequently established here with a large retinue, and it was, says Dallaway§, concerning a manor (South-Mundham) within this lordship, that a dissension originated between him and Henry II. which terminated in Becket's assassination.

The scite of the Archiepiscopal palace is very visible at a short distance from the south-east side of

* This monarch was unable for want of learning to write his name, he therefore made his cross. In one of his charters he says, "Propria manu pro ignorantia literarum signum sancti crucis expressi et subscripsi."—On account of my ignorance of letters, I have hereto expressed and subscribed my own hand by making the Holy Cross" Selden Jur. Angl. lib. i. p. 43. See also Blackstone's Comment. vol. 2, p. 305.

† Matthew Paris.

"§ South-Mundham not having formed part of the grant to the see of Canterbury, was reclaimed by Henry, who instigated John, the Mareschal of his Exchequer, to contend with Becket, the Archbishop, and to deny his jurisdiction as to this manor, and to appeal thence, to the King's Court for justice. It was the first instance in which the King openly opposed that powerful prelate. Gowan of Canterbury relates that John, the Mareschal, came into the clerk's court and swore upon a tropare or book of old songs, which he drew from under his gown." See Hume, vol. i. 397. In the 11th of that reign John de Mareschal's lordship in Pagham was assessed forty pounds in silver, in an aid for the marriage of the King's daughter.

Ibid.

the church. The irregularity of the ground, occasioned by digging up the foundations for the removal of the materials, and the wide and deep fosse by which the palace was defended, still exist; and it would not be a difficult task for an antiquarian to form a tolerably correct Ichnography of the whole, as some of the ancient wall remains undisturbed.

In tracing the scite of the old fashioned garden, I could not help fancying that I saw the marble statues, and ornamental vases of purest alabaster once there; the sun-dial too, that silent moralist, in the centre of the lawn, the latter like a carpet of emerald velvet—the sequestered valleys, formed by green wall-like hedges, neatly clipped, but leafy to the very earth,—the vistas, broad, straight, and so lengthened as to give a distant perspective to the eye, broken only by an occasional statue or fountain, where you might walk in the noonday heat fanned by the waving sprays of slender trees, and producing a moving and playful fretwork of light and shadow—and here, in fancy's eye, the grey haired and venerable archbishop perambulated and sought food for meditation and prayer! But to proceed—

The domain of Pagham was formerly of great extent. William de Pageham, tenant of the lordship under the Crown, was sheriff of the county, from the 16th to the 21st of Edward I. In the 12th of John, Richard Pageham was admitted principal tenant.

In 1104 it had the grant of a weekly market and fair.

Some time previous to, or about the year 1345, the same irruption of the sea, that carried away valuable tracts of land at Felpham and Middleton, also devastated 1700 acres of land at Pagham, from which the vicar received annually 10*l.* 10*s.* This sweeping devastation carried dismay and ruin amongst the inhabitants of this and the adjoining districts, and occasioned the present harbour of Pagham, and the estuary extending above a mile across, and rather more in length, to Sidlesham mill.

The village of Pagham lies near the harbour, at the south-western extremity of the parish. The rides are extremely pleasant, but no accommodation is offered for bathing. Those, however, Dr. Davis observes*, who may be induced to spend a few weeks on this spot, and possess sufficient strength and courage, may here commit themselves to the arms of Neptune unperceived, and with no less safety and delight than at Bognor.

The Soil is extremely fertile, and bears a decided preference in that respect to the land in the neighbourhood.

There are five tythings in this parish. 1. Nytimber and Pagham. 2. Grimsham. 3. South-Mundham. 4. Aldwick. 5. The Seven Households, and five hamlets or manor farms.

1. Nytimber now belongs to the devisees of W. Brereton, Esq. The chantry founded in the church of Pagham was endowed with lands in Nytimber.

2. Aldwick, of which a description has been given.

3. Boley or Bogheley—a very ancient manor farm, held by the tenure of knight's service, as part of the paramount manor of Boseham, and not to the Archbishop's court. In 1688 Henry Lord

* Origin and description of Bognor, p. 123.

Berkeley, in right of his manor of Boseham, recovered the wardship of Thomas Payne for this estate in the Common Pleas. It consisted at that period of 240 acres. Lawrence Alcock, Esq. of Midhurst purchased it in 1693. In 1794 it was aliened to Nathaniel Newnham, Esq. Alderman of London, and has been sold by Mrs. Newnham, his widow, to Mr. James Hack, of Chichester, Banker.

4. South-Mundham formerly belonged to William de Gardinis.(a) Afterwards it became the property of John Quantock, Esq. of Chichester, in right of his wife, Mary, daughter of Mr. Richard Heather. Another considerable estate in South-Mundham belongs to Mr. William Peachey, whose ancestors acquired it by marriage, from the family of Young.

5. Lagness, Lagnersh, or in Saxon *Legenhurst*, which belonged to the Priory of Boxgrove.

6. Grimsham, an exempted manor, held of North-Bersted. In 1665 it was held by Thomas Woodyer, Gent. in right of his wife, and was inherited by Richard Merricks, Esq. deceased, from the heir female of that family, and now belongs to his son and heir.

The Benefice is a vicarage, and within the peculiar jurisdiction of the Archbishop of Canterbury. The appropriation took place about the year 1283. In 1365 Archbishop Simon de Islyp, upon his founding Canterbury Hall, Oxford, endowed it with the great tythes of the parish; but the students having given him offence by electing Wyckliffe fellow, deprived them of this appropriation, and transferred it to the monks of

(a) The modern name is Jordan.

Canterbury, who retained it till the suppression of monasteries by Henry, when it was settled upon the Dean and Chapter*. Ultimately the impropriation was given to the master and scholars of St. John's College, Cambridge, for founding and endowing two fellowships and two scholarships to be chosen from the grammar school of Peterborough.

In 1774 a lease of two third parts of the impropriate tythes was granted by St. John's College, Cambridge, which were sold under the Land Tax Redemption Acts, in 1800, to William Brereton, Esq.

The Vicarage house was burnt down in 1703, and the registers to that period destroyed. There are two terrars of the particulars of the vicarage in the registry of the Archbishop's peculiars at Chichester, of the dates of 1626 and 1635, in one of which is the following entry:

> "The fishermen inhabiting within this parish doe pay tythe of their fishe, called Christ's share."

This tythe is not now paid.

The ruins of St. Andrew's Chapel may be traced near the vicarage house, which has of late years undergone great improvement. The Rev. Edward Goddard, Rural Dean, is the present incumbent.

THE CHURCH,

Is dedicated to St. Thomas à Becket, that proud and imperious prelate, who, in the days of the second Henry, was deemed worthy to receive the

---

* Dallaway. A Bull was obtained from Pope Urban the fifth for detaching it from the see. *Ib.* Rot. Pat: 33 Hen. VIII. Advocatio Ecclesiæ et Rectoriæ de Pagham Decano et Capitulario.

honours of canonization, soon after which event his successor caused this edifice, then recently erected, to bear his name. The church has lately been taken down and rebuilt, and greatly ornamented; but an unfortunate illness of the Editor of this work precludes him from the gratifying task of describing the improvements which have taken place. At the end of the north aisle was the chantry founded by John Bowyer and Alice his wife. To this chantry some of the inhabitants had the right of presentation, for it appears by an entry in the registry at Chichester, that William Frauncis was presented to it by the parishioners of Pagham, *as was their custom* in the year 1316*.

These chantries were commonly little chapels or particular altars, such as we see in cathedrals and other churches on the Continent, endowed with lands or revenues for the maintenance of a priest, to pray for the souls of the founder and his friends, on a supposition of purgatory, and of being released from thence by masses and prayer.

In the Cathedral at Chichester, there were as late as 1535, sixteen of these chantries, nine of which received their stipends from the Dean and Chapter, and no less than sixty-five anniversaries celebrated in that church during that year, the chief of which were for Bishop Richard de la Wich and King Henry V. The services were in some once, and in others twice, a week. But all chantries were put an end to by the statute of 1 Edward VI. c. 14, and the lands seized by the Crown and alienated to different individuals.

---

* Regist. Reynolds, fol. 25. Gulielmus Frauncis ad cantario Beatæ Mariæ Virginitatis presentatus per parochianis istius eclesiæ.

Those attached to Pagham were granted to Henry Polsted and William Moore in soccage.*

On the margin of a stone slab in the chancel, is an inscription in Lombardic characters. Some of the words and letters are obliterated, but the following appear:

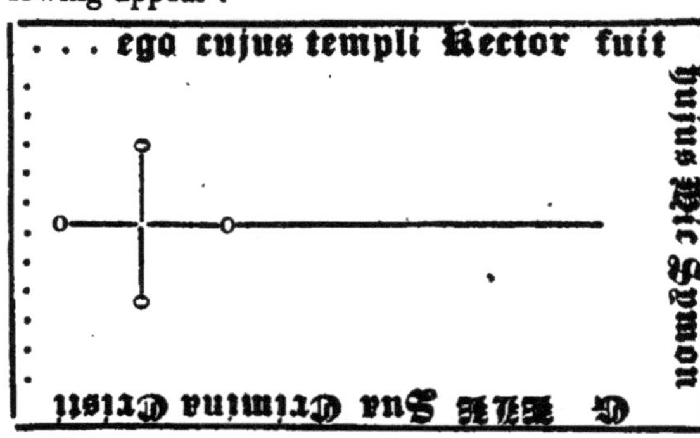

This stone was taken up a short time ago, and underneath were the bones of the Reverend person whose memory these lines were intended to perpetuate, reposing in a stone coffin, and he appeared to have been interred in his canonicals, which we must suppose was conformable to the custom of the times, as other bodies have been discovered in other churches correspondent with this.

Upon a stone in the wall the following appears,

"Edmunde Darell, Esquior, Clerk of the caterie of the Cuene's household, deceased the xxth daye of June, Anno Dni. 1573."

And on a stone in the chancel the following:

"Polyxena, wife of John Barfoot, Minister of Pagham, obit 1652."

* Dallaway. Rot. p. 2nd. Edward VI.

"Viator! Siste, precor, lege ac luge; in hoc tumulo, terræ cumulo, cum omni virtute circumlata, tumulata, jacet Polyxena; præmissa, non amissa, non enim perit qui vitam meliorem reperit." This I translate thus;

Stop traveller I pray thee! Read and be enlightened! In this tomb, entombed, in a heap of earth, heaped up with every virtue, lies Polyxena. Gone before, but not lost, for she *loses* not who *finds* a better life.

And on a marble slab,

"Here lies interred, Charlotte, eldest daughter of Sir Thomas Brooke Pechell, Bart. ob. 1802, at 12 years."

The worthy Baronet also lies buried here.

The Hissing Pool.

About the middle of Pagham harbour, and at high water, a space of 130 feet in length by 30 in breadth, presents the singular appearance of boiling, from the rushing of immense volumes of air to the surface; and the sound of the bursting of the bubbles resembles the simmering of a huge caldron. The temperature of the air was 48, of the water 44, and of the gas, as it rushed through the apertures 46. On the retreat of the tide, the bank was found to be a bed of shingle, through which the air continued to bubble as long as it remained moist. On digging a few feet and throwing water into the hole the bubbling was renewed. On analysing a specimen of the gas, it proved to be atmospheric air; but it seems difficult to explain the cause of this singular phenomenon.

To the north of Pagham are the very pleasant villages of Northmundham, the church of which is worth seeing; and Runcton, in which last is a handsome house belonging to R. Merricks, Esq.

CHAPTER X.

SELSEY.

We now enter into a most interesting portion of our work—that of Selsey; interesting not only on account of its proximity to Bognor, and of its being always in sight of the spectator, as he traverses the shore, but also on account of its ancient importance as once containing a Cathedral, and of being the place where, in the early history of the country, Christianity was established through the instrumentality of the pious and active Wilfride, who induced the inhabitants of this little peninsula, to quit the debasing rites of paganism and embrace the milder precepts and enlightening doctrines of the founder of our religion.

Wilfride, exiled from the Bishoprick of Lindisferne by Egfrid, King of the Northumbrians, in consequence of a quarrel between them, on the subject of the division of that extensive diocese into two Bishopricks, which Wilfride opposed, directed his steps towards the country inhabited by the South Saxons, and sought refuge in the court of Ædelwalch, the Sovereign of that district*. This prince received Wilfride on friendly terms, and sent him to Selsey to preach Christianity amongst his subjects there. He proceeded thither, and according to the account transmitted to us by the monkish historians of that period, his arrival was followed by the performance of a miracle—for the inhabitants of this peninsula *being entirely ignorant of the art of catching fish, except eels*, Wilfride made a net, and soon found a miraculous draught, three hundred of which he distributed amongst them, and predisposed them to receive his doctrines. This clumsy fabrication was well suited to a period when the people were entirely ignorant of the holy scriptures, but its grossness, and its assimilation to the miraculous draft of fishes in holy writ, are now sufficiently apparent.

It is not easily to be believed that an archbishop should understand how to make nets, and persons living by the sea-side all their lifetimes be ignorant of it†.

He continued at Selsey five years, and having established a monastery there, was afterwards recalled to York. It does not appear that Wilfride

* He was the sole prelate in the Northumbrian Kingdom, and appealed to Rome against the decisions of an English synod, which had abridged his diocese by the erection of some new Bishopricks.

Hume, vol. 1. p. 62, who quotes Bede and Higden.

Ædilwalch commenced his reign about the year 648, and with his wife Æle, had been baptized into the Christian faith from Paganism before the arrival of Wilfride in Sussex.

Collyer's Eccl. Hist. vol. 1. p. 108.

† Docuit Antistes Wilfridus eos piscari nam prius nisi ad anguillas piscari solebant. Collectis igitur retibus in mare misit et mox ter centum pisces cepit &c.

Dec. Scriptores p. 738, Dallaway.

at that time assumed the title of bishop, as his two successors, Hiadda in 686, and Daniel in 705, were stiled abbots.

Ædilwalch being subdued in battle by Ceadwalla King of Wessex, and slain (A. D, 686), was ultimately succeeded by the latter, not without opposition and bloodshed, in the kingdom of the South Saxons, or Sussex, which became swallowed up in the kingdom of Wessex*.

Wilfride, who had gone to Rome on the subject of his appeal respecting the division of his Diocese of Northumbria, having returned to Selsey, brought with him four priests named Eolla, Feoda, Brunela, and Oidda or Hidda; and having constituted them secular canons of his new church, he began to concert with them the establishment of a Bishoprick, over which he himself should preside.

Having in 686 succeded in converting Ceadwalla to Christianity, he obtained from that powerful prince a confirmation of Ædilwalch's charter, and a more extensive grant of lands, for the establishment of the new See of Selsey: and though the domains were of smaller extent than were afterwards obtained when the Cathedral was removed to Chichester, they were competent to the support of the new church, in those primitive and simple times, and exceeded all others in the South Saxon district with respect to fertility and number of inhabitants.

* "He entirely subdued the Kingdom of Sussex and annexed it to his own dominions.—He made inroads into Kent. ...... Tired at last with wars and bloodshed, Ceadwalla was seized with a fit of devotion, bestowed several endowments on the church, and made a pilgrimage to Rome, where he received baptism and died in 689." Hume, vol. 1. p. 55.

The Church is dedicated to St. Peter, as was the ancient Cathedral. It consists of a nave and two aisles ceiled with oak and divided by arches. It is supposed to have been built by Bishop Reade. The Tower was left unfinished at his death, and has never been completed. It is at an inconvenient distance from the village. In the pavement of the nave are inserted several coffin-shaped slabs of Sussex marble, upon which are carved flourished crosses, as used to commemorate ecclesiastics of the Saxon era. The font of black marble is circular and deep, raised upon steps and supported by a large shaft, surrounded by four small ones. These were brought from the ruins of the ancient monastery. It has no carvings. In the primitive ages of the church, baptism was acquired by total immersion, and consequently the most ancient fonts are the largest.

In the Chancel is a mural monument of Caen stone, with carved effigies of Sir John Lews, Knight, and of Agatha his wife.

Both effigies are in a kneeling posture, with hands clasped and a book before them. Near to the husband is the figure of a knight armed and plumed, his right hand supporting a lance thrust into the mouth of a dragon on which he treads, his left bearing a sword. On the side of the wife are three figures, the centre being a naked woman, apparently tied by her waist to a tree, and two men, one on each side, applying an instrument resembling a pair of scissars to her breasts. The whole monument is about five feet wide and six feet high.

As it is not probable that the Bognor visitor will be desirous of extending his excursions westward beyond Selsey, we now turn to the northward and visit Goodwood.

CHAPTER XI.

GOODWOOD.

It was anciently called Godinwood, and is mentioned in Domesday Book as a Woodland tract. It received its name from its Saxon owner "Godinus or Godwin," whose property was not forfeited at the conquest; and he himself is stiled "*Liber homo*," because not holding in demesne.

Before the year 1720, Goodwood was purchased of the family of Compton of East-Lavant, by Charles, the first Duke of Richmond, as a hunting seat, and for occasional resort, but having been greatly enlarged and modernized, it became the residence of that noble family. Its present grandeur and extent in a stile of unusual magnificence are solely due to the late Master General of the Ordnance (the 3rd. Duke) who dedicated his leisure and ample fortune to its improvement both in planting and building. The extensive park and the hills and the vallies attached to it, laid out as they are with plantations, form a beautiful and picturesque scenery; and the trees which have now attained a maturity of growth, form an additional revenue to the present Duke.

The great addition to the former mansion was begun in the year 1800. Its front is 196 feet and it faces the east. A portico of Ionic columns adorns the centre for the entrance, surmounted by a balustrade; each side of the centre is terminated by two circular towers with hemispherical roofs, which are considered as the least ornamental part of the mansion—and, from these, two wings branch off upon an angle of 45 degrees, which, as the house is viewed at a distance, has the peculiar effect of appearing in a continuous line with the centre.

There are two principal approaches to Goodwood house, one from Waterbeach, where a public house is erected for the accommodation of the public and another from the road made for the entrance of the Emperor of Russia and the Duchess of Oldenburgh, when they paid a visit to this splendid mansion in the year 1814. The whole building, with the conservatory adjoining, and the magnificent stables, the lofty and wide spreading trees in the park, whose ample branches with their rich and varied foliage, reach to the ground, and the beautiful wood called *The Highwood*, which skirt the rear, have a most imposing effect; whilst the cawing of the rooks from their leafy mansions in the air, the verdure of the carpet beneath the feet, and the salubrity of the air, give an enviable cheerfulness to the mind.

The buildings, except the old front, are uniformly of square flint stones of the neatest masonry, and the mortar which was made of ground flints, is become as hard, and will be as durable, as the flints themselves. The whole architectural design originated with the noble founder, who personally superintended its execution.

The Entrance Hall.

In entering this superb hall the visitor is struck with the beauty of six pillars of Guernsey granite, which were cut from the solid rock and brought to

Goodwood, and there polished by his Grace's workmen. The plinth and tori are composed of white and black marble nine inches high;—the shafts thirteen feet, and the Corinthian capitals, of bronze, two feet high. On a rich marble table are placed two busts, one of the Emperor Trajan, the other of Apollo of Belvidere.—The chimney pieces are of Egyptian granite, and of other marble. Trophies of victory, obtained in battle by his present Grace*, when Lord March, who has nobly fought and freely bled in the service of his country, adorn the hall. Crossing this hall, you enter

The Egyptian Drawing Room.

Its size is forty-six feet by twenty-four. The plan of the room is said to have been suggested by the discoveries of a temple and palace at Tentyra by Mons. Dinon. The walls are of Scagliola, resembling a rich polished Sienna marble, with a cornice and skirting of grey and white marble, adorned with classic ornaments in bronze. Before a superb looking-glass stands a vase of Egyptian porphyry, and on each side are small tables of choice granite. The lower end, or principal entrance of the room, forms an alcove, in which are two niches, containing busts of the third Duke of Richmond, when young and on his travels, and of the late Marquis of Rockingham, by Nollekins; near, on tables of granite and under glasses, are girandole figures of Isis and Osiris in bronze. The chimney-piece is of the finest statuary marble, adorned with bronzed Egyptian hieroglyphics; from the ceiling are suspended two elegant bronze

* His Grace was Aid-de-camp to the Duke of Wellington at the Battle of Waterloo.

and cut glass lamps. The floor is of oak wrought in marquetry, which, with the drapery and rest of the furniture, is truly unique.

In this superb room on the 24th of June, 1818, were entertained the Emperor of Russia and his sister, on their visiting Goodwood as before mentioned.

The Wainscot Library.

The size of the room is twenty-three feet eight inches by nineteen feet ten inches, and the walls are hung with scarlet flock paper. From the ceiling is suspended a lustre with bronze lamps. Access to the upper part of the library is afforded by means of a small geometrical stair-case, which leads up to a light iron gallery supported by cantalivres of the same metal, bronzed, with a top rail of mahogany, which extends nearly round the room, and has been justly admired for its elegant appearance and its strength and utility.

The Breakfast Room

Is an elegant circular apartment on the same floor of the south tower, twenty feet in diameter. The walls are hung with paper of a light blue chintz pattern, ornamented with a drapery of the same coloured silk tabinet. Two of the spaces for windows are of looking glass. From the centre of the room is suspended a glass lustre, the lights from which, when in full blaze, are reflected a thousand times in those magnificent mirrors, and remind us of the description of oriental splendour in the Arabian Nights.

The Grand Library

Is thirty-five feet seven inches by twenty-five feet six inches, and contains a large and judicious selection of Books. Around are erected lofty cases with doors of light brass wire work containing the books, &c. Beneath, from the drawings of Sir William Hamilton, are Greek, Etruscan, and Roman vases, found in the ruins of Herculaneum. The ceiling is divided into compartments, carved and gilt and adorned with paintings by Riley, in vivid colours, from those discovered in the baths of Titus at Rome. From the centre is suspended a superb bronze and gilt lamp. Over the chimney piece, which is of the finest statuary marble, is a painting inserted, descriptive of the death of Cleopatra; and above the doors to the right and left are Bacchus and Ariadne, by Riley. On the pediments of the bookcases are several busts in porphyry and other marble. The walls are of salmon colour ornamented with gold medallions and foliage in bas relief. The drapery to the windows and furniture are composed of the richest silk tabinet of the same colour. Between the windows are two looking-glasses, each nine feet three inches by five feet seven inches. Before them are tables of polished granite, and beneath are a pair of antique Thebaic vases, taken in a French frigate, and forming part of the plunder of the army of Egypt under Napoleon.

The chimney piece and granite tables are decorated with costly pieces of Sevre and other porcelain, and on each side hang highly finished miniatures in ivory, of the present Duke, of Lord George Lennox, his brother, and of the Duchess of Argyll, together with a portrait of the present Duke's father, by Scott.

The Study

Contains every requisite necessary for the accoutrement of a sportsman, and some excellent engravings.

The Great Stair-case.

The steps are of the finest polished wainscot. The walls are painted with a light drab colour, and the windows decorated with a rich full scarlet drapery. Upon a large marble stove, which communicates heat to the chief apartments in the mansion, stand some fine antique heads in marble, consisting of a Bacchus, a Naiad, &c. In a niche is a large bust of Adonis after he had received his mortal wound from the boar. Looking upwards we behold that celebrated and justly admired painting by Vandyke, of King Charles I. and family, purchased from the Orleans collection by the third Duke of Richmond for 1155*l.* The picture is nine feet nine inches by eight feet two inches, and represents the King seated with his son, Charles, Prince of Wales, resting on his knee; his Queen Henrietta, daughter of Henry IV. of France, is holding up the infant Princess Maria; two small Italian dogs are playing at their feet. On a table beside the King lie the Royal Regalia, and in the perspective may be seen Westminster Hall and the Abbey.

In the stair case may be seen other pictures of this family by the same celebrated painter. There is also a fine full length of Charles II. in his robes, by Sir Peter Lely, seven feet six inches by four feet eight inches, which is considered one of the best portraits of that great painter.

In the gallery are four of Charles's favorite mistresses by the same artist, viz. Barbara Villiers, Duchess of Cleveland, Eleanor Gwynne, Mrs. Middleton, and the beautiful Louisa de Querouaille, Duchess of Portsmouth; and over the door to the east and west are displayed half portraits of the Count and Countess Querouaille the parents of that celebrated beauty.

Near to a brilliant picture of Francis Stuart, Duchess of Richmond, the daughter of Walter Stuart, Esq*. who is arrayed as Minerva, with cuirass, helmet, and spear, is another fine full length painting of the same Louisa de Querouaille, by Sir Godfrey Kneller, the drapery supported by a black boy. The size of this portrait is seven feet nine inches by four feet ten inches.

A third painting of the same lady hangs beneath the large picture of Charles and his family.

Under the stair-case in the lower apartment of the area is a portrait of Cardinal de Fleury; and a small cabinet portrait of the second Duke of Richmond in a full black dress. The Countess of Berkeley, by *Kneller*, and Madame de France, by *Lely*.

---

*She married her namesake Charles Stuart, Earl of Lichfield, who succeeded his cousin as Duke of Richmond and Lennox in 1660, and died at Elsineur, when employed as Ambassador to the Court of Denmark, without issue. The voluptuous Charles is said to have assailed the virtue of this lady, who was possessed of uncommon beauty, with the most insidious arts, but could not succeed in the accomplishment of his wishes.

The Duchess's Boudoir

Is most elegantly fitted up, and contains portraits of the Duke and Duches of Gordon, parents of the present Duchess Dowager of Richmond. Also many excellent proof prints of celebrated public characters, and a small select library.

In the anti-room are a variety of stuffed birds in glass cases, chiefly specimens of British game.

The China Room

Is thirty-three feet by thirteen feet. This elegant apartment is well stored with a valuable collection of Dresden, Sevre and India porcelain. There are two small tables inlaid with choice specimens of minerals and marble, particularly one which has a large piece of mocha in the centre.

The Scarlet Chamber.

In size thirty-two feet by eighteen feet, is adorned with a very handsome marble chimney piece. It contains a picture of Antiochus, son of Seleucus, King of Syria, who fell in love with Stratonice his mother-in-law. Erastratus, the King's physician, discovered his malady to his father, by causing all the ladies of the palace to pass before his patient as he lay in bed; when the father, to save the life of his son, consented to their union, and made them King and Queen of Upper Asia.

Here is also a picture of St. Madeline, by Correggio, from the Dresden gallery. In the

Dressing Room

Adjoining, is a collection of portraits in crayons of the whole train of Noblemen and Gentlemen and Ladies belonging to the celebrated Goodwood Hunt. Descending to the lobby of the

Stone Stair-case,

Many valuable pictures salute the view. Of these it is not within the limits of this publication to give a particular account; and the reader should observe, that some of them may have changed their position since this work was written.

In the Waiting Room

Are two superb sets of Sevre porcelaine, one blue and gold, the other green and gold, presents from the French Court, and beautifully embellished with subjects from natural history.

Whoever has visited the Royal Manufactory of china and porcelain at Sevre, and demanded to know the prices of some of the articles there, will know how to appreciate these specimens of French art.

In this room are various family portraits, and one by *Gainsborough* of Pitt.

The Great Hall or Saloon

Next attracts our notice. It is fifty nine feet by nineteen feet three inches. Each end is supported by a row of six fluted Ionic columns, with pilasters and a modillion cornice. Over the chimney-picce are views of London by *Cannaletti*. On the walls hang portraits of some celebrated horses, by *Wotton*. In niches and various parts of this superb room, are antique heads of Nero, Caligula, a Roman Lady, a Vestal, &c. &c. On the Library tables are bronze busts of King Charles II. and Sarah, second Duchess of Richmond. In this room Divine Service is performed every Sabbath by his Grace's Chaplain, and in it are two organs.

In the Old Billiard Room

Are other family portraits, and in a bed room adjoining is a fine portrait by *Sir Godfrey Kneller* of the first Duke of Richmond, when about nine years of age, at which time this favorite youth was admitted Companion of the most noble order of the Garter—and he is represented as being clothed with the insignia of that order.

The Dining Room

Is twenty-five feet square, and partly wainscotted. On the walls are a pair of huge paintings, representing the festival held at Athens, in honour of Bacchus and Ceres. The full length portrait in the Turkish costume is of a person unknown. On the table under a glass is an original cast by *Nollekins* of Mr. Pitt, taken on the 23rd. of January, 1806, the day of his death.

In a corner of the room in a glass case, is an Egyptian mummy, five feet high. It is of a female, and was sent to England from Egypt to the third Duke of Richmond.

The State Bed Room

Is in size twenty-four feet five inches by twenty-three feet nine inches, and is adorned with Gobeline tapestry of most brilliant colours, and carefully preserved. They are in compartments representing the Four Seasons. Each is about eleven feet seven inches in height by nine feet wide. The state bedstead is of the finest mahogany, richly carved and gilt, surrounded by a kind of throne, the steps of which are covered with crimson velvet, the furniture and canopy are of the most costly velvet and satin, embroidered in gold with the arms of the noble family. A pair of looking glasses, each eight feet eight inches by five feet four inches, adorn the room. The other parts of the furniture are equally splendid. To the right is

The Dressing Room,

The ceiling of which is painted with subjects from the antique. It contains a very curious ebony cabinet, inlaid with ivory and silver; the doors and drawers are adorned with agate, japan, lapis lazuli, and other minerals.

The Drawing Room,

In which are magnificent and choice pieces of tapestry, from the Gobelin manufactory. They were presented by the French King to Charles, the third Duke of Richmond, when Ambassador, and illustrate four of the principal adventures in the History of Don Quixote: 1. Consulting the Brazen Head, fourteen feet three inches by twelve feet. 2. Mambrino's Helmet, nine feet two inches by twelve feet. 3. Don Quixote fastened to the window, by Maritorno. The Adventure at the Inn with the Chambermaid, seventeen feet by eleven feet ten inches.

The marble chimney piece most exquisitely sculptured, containing Venus and Adonis as drawing aside a drapery to unveil the fire-place, is considered as the *chef d'œuvre* of the late Mr. John Bacon.

The size of the room is thirty-five feet three inches by twenty-three feet eight inches. The ceiling, cornice and mouldings are richly carved and gilt. The floor is covered with a magnificent carpet of English manufacture. The sofa and chairs are covered with white satin, richly embossed in various colours. Over the chimney is inserted a very large looking-glass, of a single plate, eight feet eight inches by five feet four inches, and there are three others in other parts of the room of a still larger size.

At each end of the apartment stands a large table, one of *Verd antique*, the other of choice granite. On one of them is a pair of alabaster vases and a costly buhl time-piece; and on the other a fine bust of the Duke of Wellington by *Turnville*, and another of the late Mr. Pitt by *Nollekins*. Beneath them are a large red porphyry basin and a pair of superb china jars.

Near the door, which is wrought in mahogany, ebony, and satin wood embossed with carving, stands a japan folding screen, and a rich buhl cabinet, with drawers inlaid with tortoiseshell, on which are small busts in marble of George III. by *Tourneille*, and of the late Duchess of Devonshire by *Nollekins* from a cast by *Mrs. Damer*.

Among other curiosities here kept, is a model of a Chinese house, a shirt of Charles I. and the cup, boat, and salver used at the birth of Charles II. A beautiful view of the dog kennels presents itself from the window of this room, which, with the intervening lawn, forms a most pleasing *coup d'œil*.

As no description of Goodwood House and of the works of art it contains was ever published before Mr. Jaques's time, and as his work is in very few hands, and is out of print, this account, taken in great part from his "Visit to Goodwood," cannot but be acceptable to those persons who may be disposed, during their sojourn at Bognor, to take an excursion to this fairy spot. But our description must not rest here.—We must now proceed to that sequestered grove, sacred to solitude, The High Wood.

Of the stable, however, near to the house, we must first say a few words. It is a handsome quadrangular building, from a design of Sir William Chamber, capable of containing fifty-four horses, with rooms above for grooms and stable keepers. Adjoining are extremely convenient offices and workshops, of unique and chaste designs, the exterior being of square flint, and having a particularly cheerful appearance.

The High Wood.

This is a tract of land behind the house of about forty acres, laid out with singular felicity of taste. The mossy walks, the lofty and venerable trees, the "alleys green," the cool shades, the awful silence that pervades around, uninterrupted only by the cawing of the rooks, or the more tuneful harmony of others of the feathered race, who seek an asylum in this lone retreat, excite in the mind the most pleasing sensations—and if any should enter into this wood with perturbed and ruffled feelings, they must soon find them calmed and smoothed down to a state of tranquillity and repose.

" I love amid these deep embowered dells,
These silent grottos, and these shady cells,
These subterranean caves, by Fancy made,
And Hermitage, deep hid amid the shade,
I love throughout these 'alleys green' to stray,
Secluded from the garish eye of day.

In this place we are naturally attracted to a temple, raised on an artificial mound of earth, that contains one of the oldest inscriptions in Britain. It was found at Chichester, in digging the foundations for the erection of the present Council Chamber in the North Street. It is supposed to have been part of an ancient temple, erected in the time of Tiberius Claudius, and dedicated, as the inscription shews, to Neptune and Minerva, by a company of Roman artificers, then resident at Chichester, the Regnum of that people. Claudius conquered Britain (Augustus Cæsar having only achieved a partial conquest); and as Claudius crossed the sea in safety from Gaul to Britain, and had a triumph decreed to him for his conquest of this country, a dedication of the temple to Neptune, the God of the sea, conceived by these pagans to have been propitious to his voyage, and to Minerva, the Goddess of Wisdom, for its happy results, was appropriate enough. Cogidubnus, a British chief, but friendly to the Romans, had been invested with kingly power over Sussex, and he is therefore, in this inscription, said to have authorised the erection of the temple, and Pudens, the son of Pudentinus, one of the followers of the Romans, and one to whom for his bravery or fidelity land had been allotted, to have given the ground.

The stone was broken through the carelessness of the workmen in taking it up, and part only of the inscription is visible. It is about four feet in length, three feet broad, and between two and three inches thick, and for its great antiquity is certainly an object of great curiosity, and considered as the oldest Roman inscription in Britain*.

* The stone, if erected in the temple at the time of Claudius, must be about 1800 years old, as Claudius was living in A. D. 14. This Emperor was the son of Livia, wife of Augustus,

In the ORANGERY, a little beyond the temple, is one of the largest tulip trees (*tulip fora, arbor virginiana*) in the kingdom. It is a native of North America, and in Carolina is said to grow to the size of thirty feet in circumference, and to the height of seventy or eighty feet. This tree was planted in the year 1739, and in the months of July and August is covered with a profusion of flowers.

In the front are the figures of two men cast in lead, contending in mortal fight, supposed to be Cain and Abel.

In the centre of the wood is a romantic spot, with ruined buildings, in imitation of destruction by an earthquake—with grottos of shell-work, formed for cemeteries of some favorite animals of the family, with curious inscriptions—Here is also a subterranean passage, and an hermitage with an open stone coffin at the entrance, as a memento of mortality.

The Dairy

Is a very beautiful building, representing the interior of a gothic temple; the roof is formed of carved oak, and the buttresses are terminated by angels bearing shields, inscribed with the arms of Lennox, Querouaille, Brudenell, and Cadogan. The windows are formed of various pieces of

---

by Tiberius Nero. The quaint Prideaux says "he made himself shy in undertaking the charge of the empire, *but entering like a Fox, reigned like a Lion, and died like a Dog.* He was called, on account of his vices. Tiberius Nero, *Caldius Biberius Mero*. He was suspected to have been concerned in making away with Marcus Agrippa, the right heir to Augustus."

ancient coloured glass, Emerging from this enchanting spot, we re-enter the park and proceed to the

Dog Kennel,

Which, for extent and arrangement, is unequalled by any other in England destined for the same purpose, and forms a pleasing termination to the view from the mansion house. It was erected by the third Duke, under the superintendence of Mr. James Wyatt. The distribution of the building is into four kennels and two feeding rooms, in each of which is a ventilator, and stoves to warm them in winter or air them in damp weather.

There is a constant supply of rain water from a reservoir beneath, that contains seven thousand hogsheads, the whole of which can be drained off.

There are two airing yards with tanks of water for the use of the dogs,—In the north wing are breeding rooms and a boiling house, with other conveniences.

For the use of the huntsman are two good parlours, two kitchens, and four sleeping rooms, with a two stalled stable. To the north of the dog kennel are two cottages for the whippers in.

The Park

Is very extensive, and about six miles in circumference, and contains upwards of twelve hundred acres. At Cairney Seat, country parties are permitted to take their refreshments, and during summer scarcely a day passes without. From this spot the views are bounded only by the ocean.

Near to Cairney Seat is an unique retreat called *The Pheasantry*, where gold and silver pheasants and the common English one, as well as partridges are bred. This spot was formerly a chalk-pit, and nothing but the most consummate taste could have formed such a paradise as this out of a place of that description.

The Bee Orchis.

On a bank near to the dog kennel, and in the woods of the Valdoe, is the *Ophrys apifera*, or *Bee Orchis*. This beautiful and singular plant forms an exact representation of the bee, even to the eyes. In its last stage of existence it more resembles a dove with outstretched wings. It flowers in June and July, and then displays a singular and beautiful contrivance for its preservation. The nectarium or honey gland of the orchis is formed with so near a resemblance to the wall bee as, at a small distance, to be easily mistaken for that insect, by which appearance it is probable a number of little depredators, which are ever on the wing in search of that liquid, and which would otherwise rob the plant of its means of support, are deterred from approaching it. Other orchis's are found in the Valdoe.

CHAPTER XII.

BOXGROVE OR BOXGRAVE.

Every lover of antiquity should visit this beautiful Church. It is of very remote antiquity, and part of an ancient priory or monastery, founded as early as the year 1100 or thereabouts, by Robert de Haia, Lord of Halnacre, in the reign of Henry I. and dedicated to the Virgin Mary and St. Blase, for three monks of the Benedictine order, afterwards increased to fifteen.

In the year 1535 the priory was seized by the Crown, with all its manors and demesne lands, which extended into the parishes of Boxgrove, Mundham, Hunston, Hampnett, Birdham, and Itchenor.

The rapacious Henry, who accomplished the work of suppressing conventual and monastic bodies, sold the estates under them to the best bidders, or to favorites—and many pious persons of that era, instead of pulling down these sacred places for the sake of the materials, permitted them to remain, and gave them up for the use of the parishioners for the celebration of Divine Service.

Such was the case of the Church of Boxgrove, and the goods and furniture of the Priory, which were purchased by Sir Thomas West, Lord De La War, who was possessed of the Lordship of Halnaker, and who must have been anxious to preserve the church from destruction, he having in the year 1532 erected a sacellum or chapel in this church. It is situated on the right of the altar, and is constructed of Caen stone, most elaborately carved, painted and gilt. The length is fourteen feet, the width nine feet eight inches, and the height twelve feet.

The ancient parochial church was the nave, which from its remains was evidently of more remote antiquity than the choir. The nave retains a low arcade only left as a ruin. The choir and semi-transept are still perfect. The small chapter-house at the end of the north transept may be traced by a careful inspection. A door way with three Norman arches opened into the cloister, which extended to the refectory and the habitation of the monks. The tower is very low above the roof, which is of the era of Henry II.

The present church consists of a nave and chancel without division. These were anciently the choir. There are also two aisles. The south transept is imperfect, and the north was ceiled with a flat timber frame and otherwise altered in the reign of Henry VII.

The eastern window has three large lights, separated in the interior by tall marble shafts and flourished capitals, and externally has the nail-headed moulding. This mixture of ornamental parts is a proof that the structure is of the date of Stephen or Henry I. or Henry II. when the round Norman arch was abandoned and several novelties were introduced, which prevailed only in a few instances and for a short time. On the left side of the altar are subsellia or niches in carved stone, in which the Prior and his assistants sat during the celebration of high mass. The floor is paved with glazed tiles, finished with grotesque figures and scrolls, but without cognizances or armorial devices, which were afterwards common.

The painting and preparing these tiles for the kiln was among the employments of the monks, in which they eventually excelled. At the end of the north aisle a chantry was fitted up in the reign of Henry VI. Architecture resembling that in the aisles of Christchurch Cathedral, Oxford, may be traced in this part of the building.

The beautiful chapel erected by Thomas, Lord De La War, does not appear to have been designed for a burial place, though the inscription underneath seems to denote it.

Several sepulchral monuments in this church are worthy of some investigation. There are six of them, all consisting of large cists, covered with slabs of Petworth marble, and under arcades of open quatrefoils, or of similar figures, and ornamented with crockets.

Philippa, wife of Lord Poynings, lies buried under a tomb on the north side of the altar. Upon the key-stone of one of the tombs are carved the arms of the family of St. John.

The interior of the church has a striking effect from the harmony of its parts with its proportions. Scarcely a fragment remains of the stained glass which once adorned the windows.

CHAPTER XIII.

VARIOUS EXCURSIONS.

A VERY pleasant excursion for the visitor is from Bognor, through Felpham, thence to Yapton, (passing by Mr. Prime's handsome house) to Avisford Hill, the seat of Sir Thomas Reynell, Bart. Turn on the right at the top of the hill, near to the "Royal Oak Inn," to Arundel, or on the left towards Chichester, or passing by a small public house called Ball's Hut, proceed homeward by turning on the left hand road through Westergate, Shripney, and South Bersted: or, at the top of Avisford Hill, instead of going to Arundel, cross the road and proceed over Slindon Common to Slindon, the seat of the Countess of

Newburgh, and Dale Park, (Madehurst Parish) the magnificent house built by the late Sir George Thomas, Bart. some time since sold to Mr. Kemp, M. P. who transferred the same to Mr. Smith, M. P. Banker, London. After this, proceed homeward by a short lane from Slindon Common immediately opposite Ball's Hut, as before.

We shall describe the places above-mentioned in the order named.

1. YAPTON.

THIS village lies on the direct road to Arundel.

The Church has a nave and two aisles, divided by a double arcade, alternately round and octangular, with capitals in foliage, of the stile prevalent in the reign of Henry III. At the west end of the aisle is a low tower. The chancel has been rebuilt and modernized. Both with respect to shape and antiquity, the font is of great curiosity, it is composed of black granite and certainly Saxon.

Yapton Bells. 1. Largest, "Thomas Warfield me BK. 1617." 2. "Ave Maria +." 3. "Samuel Knight cast mee 1712." 4, Stephen Rogers C W (Churchwarden) 1712."

The church was ceiled in 1726. Gallery at west end erected in 1730.

The pillars between the body and aisles are ornamented with sculptural devices.

The BENEFICE is a Vicarage in the Deanery of Arundel, endowed with the tithe of hay and all small tithes. There is no manse, the Vicar residing at Walberton; but it has eighteen acres of glebe, one field of which, was so fertile, that for eighteen years in succession, it had produced corn without measure—indeed the whole of Yapton is singularly fertile.

Yapton was originally called ***Yabeton.***

In the early centuries, it was subdivided by grants into parcels to several monastic bodies. But the paramount manor remained vested in the Earls of Arundel.

Richard, Earl of Arundel, upon his founding the College of Arundel, bequeathed the Manor of Balsham (Bilsom) and Yabeton, together with the impropriation and advowson of the Vicarage to the Master and Fellows.

There was formerly a manor in Yapton called ***Shulbrude Manor***, or ***Wallinchmere***, parcel of a priory there, now belonging to Inigo Thomas, Esq. who has other property in this parish.

Bilsom in Yapton.

Bilsom was originally a hamlet and chapelry. Bilsom farm containing 190 acres is held in jointure by Ann, Countess Dowager of Newburgh, and the Corporation of Chichester have 600 acres of land in Bilsom and Yapton.

WALBERTON.

Adjoining Yapton on the north is the very pleasant village of Walberton, a name demonstrative of a military station, being derived from the Saxon Vael-burg-ton:—or the town with a walled fortress or castle. The church has a nave, two aisles, and a spacious chancel with a turret of shingle at the west end, originally built as early as the thirteenth century, but the arcade has been re-erected with coarse architecture. There are no monumental inscriptions deserving of notice.

The benefice is a vicarage in the Deanery of Arundel and once appropriated to Boxgrove Priory*. It is consolidated with the village of Yapton, and has one third part of the tithes of the parish, with 24 acres of glebe.

Avisford Place.

Further on to the north is Avisford Place, the late residence of General Sir William Houston, Baronet, now of Sir Thomas Reynell, Baronet. This was formerly the family mansion and estate of Thomas Fowler, Esq. father of William Leeves, Esq. of Tortington, and was by his brother, the late Thomas Fowler, eldest son and heir of his father, sold to Sir George Montague, G. C. B. Admiral of the Red, who greatly improved and enlarged it. The scite is beautifully elevated above the maritime level, and commands a very extensive prospect.

Roman Remains at Avisford Place.

In a field belonging to this estate near Avisford House, a discovery was made in the year 1817 of a Roman Sepulchre, the particulars of which are related by Mr. Dallaway. It originated in the circumstance of making a hole with an iron crow-bar in the earth, for the purpose of setting up hurdles to enclose sheep, which bar met with repeated resistance, at about six inches deep. This induced the man, with assistance, to clear away

---

* Regist. Epis. B 102, Appropriatio et Vicariæ ordinat. Regist. Sherborne, E 86.

the surface, when they perceived a stone, similar to the gritt stone found near Petworth: it measured in length four feet, in breadth one foot eight inches, and eight inches thick, forming the covering of a solid stone chest or coffer; which being taken off, the inside proved to be neatly hollowed out in an oblong square, nearly four feet in length, and eighteen inches deep; the sides of the coffer were four inches in thickness. The objects which presented themselves consisted of pottery of the coarse light red kind, and colour of common flower pots. There were two red earthen basins, the size of large breakfast cups, and placed in saucers; six plates of the same coarse ware, the size of dessert plates; nine others smaller, two earthen candlesticks, six inches high; two earthen jugs of a globular shape, eight inches in diameter, with a tea-pot shaped handle attached to them, and a narrow neck that would not admit a finger; another jug of the same kind, with a handle and spout like a cream pot.

In a circular saucer, engrailed all round, the edge, and with a handle, was placed a smooth oval pebble, very hard, of the colour and transparency of a white currant, and of the size and exact shape of a pigeon's egg. In another saucer of the same coarse ware, was placed a black hard stone, perfectly round, the size of a nutmeg. Another saucer contained a flat oyster shell; near to which was a dish containing a thin glass lachrymatory, the size and shape of a bergamot pear, with two small glass handles. In four of the smaller dishes was a fragment of a bone, of a chalkish calcined white; but the most beautiful object that stood in the centre of this service of ancient crockery, consisted of an elegant flat bottomed square glass bottle, twelve inches high, by eight inches broad, of a light transparent sea-green colour, very thick, and nearly full of calcined bones: this bottle had a handle attached to one of the sides, and fastened to a circular neck, about two inches and a half high, the opening of which neck would scarcely admit the hand of a child into the bottle: this handle was beautifully reeded. At the end of this coffer at the corners, were two inverted conic brackets, each stood upon an earthen lamp, coarsely designed and executed. At the bottom at the other end, was a pair of sandals, apparently for a small foot, studded all over the heels and soles with hexagonal-headed brass nails, placed similarly to those in countrymens' shoes. The subjects, except the sandals, are all perfect, and without stain, and appear as when new; they are all made of the same kind of ware, and are about twenty-eight in number. Neither coins or inscriptions have been found in or near this extraordinary deposit,—The glass vase is a perfect specimen.

These curious remains are preserved in Avisford.

The first date of the Register in Yapton parish is 1556.

SLINDON.

Proceeding from Avisford Hill in a northerly direction across the Arundel and Chichester road, the visitor will soon reach the very beautiful village of Slindon, the seat of the Countess of Newburgh. It is situate on an eminence, and has a most commanding prospect of sea and land.

Slindon (supposed to be the Celindunum of the Romans) is within the Rápe of Chichester, and the hundred of Aldwick, and is one of the peculiars of the Archbishop of Canterbury and is distant from Chichester about seven miles.

The Church, always the first object of attention, is small and of ordinary architecture, consisting of a nave and two aisles, with a low obtuse spire of shingles. In thc chancel, under a niche, is the figure of a man carved in Irish oak, represented in armour of Henry the Eighth's time, with his head bare and resting on his helmet. It is attributed, but without certainty, to Anthony Kempe, one of the ancestors of the late Earl of Newburgh. On a slab of black marble is an inscription to Edward Long, Esq. born August 23rd. 1734, and died March 13th. 1813. He was the author of the History of Jamaica, a work highly esteemed.

Slindon House.

This elegant and splendid mansion was erected on the site of the ancient archiepiscopal residence, by Sir Garret Kempe, the son of the original grantee, early in the reign of Queen Elizabeth. By its subsequent proprietors it has been in part rebuilt, and fitted up according to the prevailing taste of the different ages; and from the late Earl of Newburgh it received alterations and embellishments which give it a decided claim to be ranked amongst the most eligible seats of the county. Among the family portraits in the house are 1. Sir Garret Kempe, Knt. said to have been taken at the age of 102. 2. Lady Mary Tudor, natural daughter of Charles II. who was the Countess

Derwentwater, a whole length in the dress of the court. 3, James Ratcliffe, the unfortunate Earl of Derwentwater, her son, three quarters, 1714. There is a portrait of the Beggar of Antwerp, exquisitely finished by *Myers*. The fellow to it was destroyed by the fire at Lord Montague's at Cowdray.

The ancient house was first built by an Archbishop, about the middle of the thirteenth century, and appropriated for a summer residence. Stephen Langton, Archbishop (memorable for the part he took relative to Magna Charta), died here in 1228. This residence was a favorite retirement of most of the Archbishops, till the final alienation of it, by virtue of an exchange between Cranmer and King Henry VIII. in 1453. The last possessor, Anthony James Ratcliffe, Earl of Newburgh, died on the 28th. of November, 1814, without issue, and by his will bequeathed a life interest in this estate to Anne his Countess, with remainder to Francis Eyre, Esq. of Hessop, in the county of Derby. Her ladyship now resides at the house.

The Manor of Slindon.

Slindon is described in Domesday as "Eslindune," and the manor as part of the estates of Earl Roger, granted by the conqueror. Having reverted to the crown in consequence of attainder, King Henry I. conferred it upon Anselm, Archbishop of Canterbury, and it was annexed to the lordship and Hundred of Pagham (since called Aldwick.)

MADEHURST, DALE PARK, &c.

FROM Slindon is a pleasant ride to Dale Park House, erected by the late Sir George Thomas, Bart. at an immense expence, and now the property of Mr. Smith. The house is situate on a rising ground, peculiarly favorable for commanding an unbounded sea and extensive land view. The design was from Bononi, an Italian architect. It was begun in 1784 and finished in four years. The rooms are numerous, spacious and well arranged, and the stile of architecture suitable to the taste of modern times. The whole parish is contained in the manorial estate, and comprises altogether, including the down, 2000 acres.

The vicarage of Madehurst is in the Deanery of Arundel.

The Register commences in 1639. The present Vicar is the Rev. William Stephen Bayton. The church contains nothing worthy of notice.

EARTHAM.

ABOUT a mile or two from Slindon lies the picturesque and beautiful village of EARTHAM, lately the residence of the poet Hayley, and now, in an enlarged and improved state, the abode of Mrs. Huskisson. It was purchased in 1743 by Thomas Hayley, Esq. of Chichester, of the heirs of Sir Thomas Fagg, Bart. Dedicating his leisure hours to literary pursuits, the author of "Serena" here cultivated his talents, and here he had the supreme pleasure of enjoying the society of his revered and respected friend Cowper, in his happier hours, ere he was attacked by that morbid melancholy that preyed upon and almost destroyed his finely attuned mind. Few places of similar extent can boast of more varied and extensive views than the mansion and grounds we are describing. Several points command very beautiful and enlarged prospects, where woods sweep over the acclivities of the down, and in front a diversified and rich tract of country is bounded by the sea and the Isle of Wight.

"The living is a vicarage and a ***prebendary*** to the church at Chichester." The chancel is neat.

"Against the east wall of the church on the right hand of the Communion table is erected an oval white marble monument, with the following inscription:

"Juxta hoc marmor requiescit,
Cum filio infante,
THOMAS HAYLEY; Armiger
Vir liberalis admodum at benevolus:
His, quos in vita fidissime colebat
In sepulchro iterum conjuncta est
Maria Hayley
Uxor inculpabilis, parens amantissima
Hoc qualecunque monumentum
Patri
Quem parvulus amisit
Et matri
Quæ vidua
Infantibus solicite semper invigilans
Utriusque parentis officio fungebatur
Filius consecravit
Filius, quem solum illa superstitem
'Visceribus totis, animoque complexa fovebat',
MDCCLXXV."

A marble monument by Flaxman records the death of Thomas Hayley, son of the poet.

THE BENEFICE is part of the Deanery of Boxgrave, and was anciently a parochial Prebend in the Cathedral of Chichester.

The vicarage house was built by George Ayme, Vicar, with the materials bought from the Bishop's Manor of Aldingbourne, which had been dilapidated by the parliamentary soldiers in 1643.

The Soil is of chalk, and in the better land of marle and sand.

Long Down, an insulated hill, rises in the centre of the parish, where the village is situated.

The Register of the parish commences in 1558. The Terrars to be found in the Bishop's Registry at Chichester, are of the dates of 1615 and 1635.

CHAPTER XIV.

ARUNDEL CASTLE.

The date of the castle as a military strong hold, has by some been referred to times in which the Romans were masters of this island.

Whether it was a military port at the time of the Romans or not, its architecture, according to the opinion of Edward King, author of Monumenta Vetusta, indicates at least a Saxon origin from the herringbone masonry in the walls, This we know for a certainty, that it was conferred, to gether with the Earldom of Arundel, on Roger de

Mont Gomeri, by William the Conqueror, after the Battle of Hastings, the successful termination of which gave him a whole kingdom to bestow. This Earl, so frequently mentioned in the history of the times, was Earl of Alençon, and "governed the second company of the rerewarde of the battaile of William the Conqueror, after the death of Harolde."

The circumference of the whole scite of the castle is 950 feet by 250, inclosing five acres and a half, but, with its apendages, said to have been formerly a mile in circumference; and the walls are from three to twelve feet in thickness. The ground plan nearly resembles that of Windsor Castle. It has a circular keep, in the middle, raised on a mount, partly natural but chiefly artificial, and the elevation is not dissimilar to that royal abode.

Almost in the centre of the inclosed fortification a mount is thrown up, the summit of which from the depth of the fosse is 110 feet on one side, and 80 on the other, which proudly overlooks the whole castle, and is a conspicuous object from the surrounding country. It is from eight to ten feet thick, and strengthened with ribs or buttresses. The original entrance was made through a Norman keep, now inaccessible, with a carved door case, of the common zig-zag mouldings. This keep was formerly called Beaumont's Tower, and was accessible from within and without the castle area, but was tenable independently of it. By the steps and sally port it is connected with the great gateway, which is a plain circular arch, under a large square tower, in which are two chambers, which were originally those of state, in which the Empress Maude was received. It is probable that the above constituted the whole inhabited part of the castle, when it was held by Robert de Belesmo, against Henry I. in 1102, and at the siege by King Stephen, thirty-two years afterwards. The outward gateway, which is a continuation of the first, was added by Richard Fitz Alan, in the reign of Edward I. The arches form an obtuse angle, and are ribbed and flanked by two square towers. This has been called Bevis's Tower, with a legend of its having been the residence of that champion, when porter of the castle. The barbican tower rises from an artificial mound on the north-west side of the great vallation and mount of the keep. An approach to it was practicable only by a very steep flight of steps, and a small sharply-arched door way. It was connected with the sally-port of the keep by a covered way, and the wall which surrounded the whole fortified space. This walled inclosure was strengthened by numerous square towers, open within side, and the whole embattled, and having steps to facilitate a communication around the whole circuit. *A curious military contrivance may still be seen, which is to convey sound by means of a circular funnel made through the grouted mortar in the thickness of the wall.* The last mentioned tower was originally one of the most lofty of the castle, consisting at least of four stories or divisions of chambers. Having been dismantled in the last seige, under Cromwell, it was repaired with a temporary roof, as it now remains.

The *external* gateway, under which you now pass, was fortified by a portcullis and drawbridge over the vallum or deep ditch. It was built by Richard Fitz Alan, the third Earl of that *family* but the first of that name, in the reign of Edward I.

after his return from the Welch and Scotch wars. These towers were much defaced by the effects of a battery placed upon the roof of the church by the parliamentary forces in 1643-5, and marks of cannon-shot are still visible on the walls.

The Great Hall was situate on the western side of the court, and was built by Richard, Earl of Arundel, after the French wars in the reign of Edward III. This Richard bequeathed to his son and heir "the great suit of arras (tapestry) which used to be placed in the chamber of state at Arundel."

Henry Fitz Alan, the last Earl, gave a magnificent fete in it at Christmas, 1525.

In the centre of the court yard is a well of great depth, now covered over. Under the exterior gateway are constructed small vaults, in which prisoners of war were frequently confined till their ransom was paid, and are systematically contrived to excite horror, by the exclusion of light and air.

During the lapse of five centuries, the castle suffered nothing from hostile violence, but remained the peaceful and almost constant residence of the noble owners, by whom it was gradually increased and splendidly furnished. But in 1397 it was the scene of a memorable confederacy against the weak and profligate government of King Richard II. the object of which was to sieze the King and the Dukes of Lancaster and York, and commit them to prison. Thomas of Woodstock, the King's uncle, was their chief, and they soon proceeded to acts of severity, by beheading Sir Simon Burley and others of the King's favorites. Their designs being disclosed to the King by the Earl of Arundel's son-in-law (Earl Marshall) the conspiracy terminated in the trial and execution of Richard Earl of Arundel, one of their body.

At the time of the execution of the Duke of Norfolk in 1572, the walls were universally embellished with movable tapestry, and the beds with cushions and carpets, for the tables and seats were richly embroidered with silk and gold. In such a state we may presume the castle to be until the departure of Thomas, Earl of Arundel, for the Continent in 1642.

The Earldom having descended to Philip Howard, son and heir of Thomas, Duke of Norfolk, who married Mary Fitz Alan, daughter of Henry Fitz Alan, the last Earl of that name, who died in 1579, upon his unfortunate attainder in 1585, commissioners were appointed to make a return of the castle into the exchequer. The inventory is preserved among the papers of the Lord Treasurer Burleigh, and is a document of singular curiosity. It describes not only the number of principal apartments, but the furniture they contained both for use and ornament. We are there minutely informed of all that constituted the internal magnificence of a great nobleman's palace at that period, and which was preserved with the greatest care to descend to generations in succession.

As a military position this castle was of the greatest importance, and the possession of it was gained by the Royalists and Parliamentarians alternately.

In the winter of 1643-4 it stood a siege by Sir William Waller, of seventeen days, and then having capitulated, it was given up to plunder. The walls were diminished, were dismantled on the north-west side, the great hall and the adjoining buildings were destroyed, and the whole rendered no longer a suitable residence for its noble owners.

Mr. Dallaway, in his very valuable work so often alluded to, has given the particulars of the siege, as copied from a rare pamphlet in Ant. à Woods Library, at the Ashmolean Museum, Oxford, but it is too long to insert here. It appears that Sir William Waller, and his colleague, Col. Browne, though of the fanatical party, possessed more gallantry than one would have expected, from the prevailing spirit of the age. The besieged, the account says, began to be pinched with famine, "and thereupon sent a message to Sir William Waller, desiring a treaty, by means of three persons from either party, and that the Lady Bishop with her daughters and waiting gentlewomen might have liberty to come forth and refresh themselves, to all which Sir Willam agreed, and invited the said Lady and her gentlewomen, together with Col. Bamfield, Major Bovile, and a captaine, being the persons sent from the castle, to dine with him, who had all noble respect and good entertainment*."

The account proceeds to state, that as no terms were come to, the persons on either side returned, "*but the gentlewomen continued with Sir William, who feasted and entertained them that night*; and that that afternoon the Lady Goring and her daughters came to visit the Lady Bishop

* The Lady Bishop (Byshoppe) here alluded to was the wife of Sir Edward Byshoppe, 2nd. Baronet of that name, of Parham and Enfield, in Sussex. She was 3rd. daughter of Nicholas Tufton, first Earl of Thanet, by Lady Frances Cecil, daughter of Thomas, first Earl of Exeter. Their son Thomas was wounded during the siege. Frances, their second daughter, was the wife of Henry Goring, of Highdean, afterwards a Baronet, and at this time only sixteen years old, and newly married.

and her daughter, one of them being married to Lady Goring's only son, he being in the castle, ***which visit gave a speedy accomplishment to our designs***, for Mistress Goring, after some conference with her mother-in-lawe, returned to her husband, and shortlie after the enemy sent a drum and Col. Rawlins, and Major Mullins, to treat for a final agreement, upon which treaty they condescended to Sir William." The substance of which treaty was that "all the enemies should be surrendered prisoners with the castle; all their arms, ammunition, treasure, and whatsoever they possessed into the custody and disposing of Sir William, by nine of the clock on the Saturday morning."

The celebrated Dr. Chillingworth was one of the prisoners.

The modern state of the Castle.

We quit with great reluctance the extremely interesting particulars detailed by Mr. Dallaway, of the capture of the castle, and his numerous anecdotes and laborious researches respecting the several branches of this noble family, and proceed to a description of the modern state of the castle.

Charles the late Duke of Norfolk, on coming into possession of Arundel Castle, determined to repair the dilapidation it had undergone, by the ravages of the civil war, and the lapse of time.

The square tower at the south-east angle was first built, and was begun in 1791, and the north front in 1795.

The chief front is of Portland stone, and the entrance by a large door case, upon the early Norman model; a stile which pervades the basement story.

On the west wing is a representation, in stone cement, equal to the finest sculpture, of King Alfred receiving the report of a jury, an institution first established in his reign. The entire interior of the castle is fitted up with an effect particularly characteristic and magnificent, and almost every decoration consists of the richest mahogany. And it was the design of the late Duke to floor all the principal rooms with the same costly material, but the intention was afterwards abandoned.

The Library.

The south-eastern side is principally occupied by the library, and is 122 feet in length. Externally it is of plain gothic architecture of the age of Henry VI. It is a beautiful room, admirably calculated for the purpose, and capable of holding ten thousand volumes, and all of easy access. In it was kept a judicious selection of books of general literature, and especially of classics.

The Baron's Hall.

Was begun in 1816, and is connected with a chapel at the north end. A Norman arcade forms the basement upon which it rises, and supports a paved walk towards the court, from which it is approached on the outside. Upon the frieze are carved in stone, cognizances of the family. The style of the windows and battlements is that of the fourteenth century.

The roof is of Spanish chesnut, most curiously wrought and finished, so as to produce a grand effect. The corners describe a semi-octagon. The dimensions are 70 feet by 34 feet, and 36 feet 6 inches to the centre of the roof. A skirting of mahogany encloses the room to the height of four feet. The ceiling is of oak, elaborately carved in the style of the fifteenth century.

The series of stained glass windows, which consist of thirteen, and chiefly by Backler, offers a peculiar and interesting exhibition. The largest represents the compelled ratification of Magna Charta by King John. The other personages are Baron Fitz Walter (*being a portrait of the late Duke*) attended by his page (*portrait of Henry Howard Jun. Esq.*), and by the Mayor of London (*portrait of Harvey Christian Combe, Esq. formerly Lord Mayor*), The master of the Templars, Cardinal Pandolph, the Pope's Legate, and Langton, Archbishop of Canterbury. The scene is the King's Camp at Runnimede, covered with the opposed forces of the King and Barons, with a view of Windsor Castle. Pandolph seems to examine the charter with looks of silent indignation. Langton is turning his head in conversation with other prelates behind him. Fitz Walter, the champion of his country, with a sturdy aspect is placed immediately before the King, habited in chain armour, the warlike costume of the thirteenth century. His deportment is erect and noble, his head uncovered, and there is a stern inflexibility in his countenance. His firm and dignified manner form a striking contrast with the page bearing his helmet. Without paying the slightest attention to the address of the Archbishop, his looks and mind seem wholly absorbed in the contemplation of the grand object of the assembly. Those of the King indicate great reluctance at the deed he is about to sign, and whilst his hand unwillingly performs the office, his eyes are directed towards Fitz Walter.

The twelve windows round the room are occupied by figures of barons at full length, in chain armour, and helmets closely fitted to the head, without plumes, which was the military costume of that age.

The armorial bearings of the Barons from whom the Dukes of Norfolk lineally descend, are emblazoned on their surcoats and shields. The heads represent individuals of the Howard family, at different periods of life, as the Barons who thus obtained the great charter of our liberties.

This magnificent room was opened on the 15th. of June, 1815, and a splendid entertainment given in commemoration of the sixth century on that day completed. At this sumptuous dinner a numerous suite of the nobility and gentry of the county attended: among them were twenty-two individuals of the four branches of the Howard family, and probably more than ever met together at one table since they had obtained the first rank of nobility. The vast display of ancient plate and certain baronial ceremonies rendered this a scene of splendour rarely exhibited.

At this banquet his Majesty Geo. IV. (then Prince Regent) with several of his royal brothers were the expected guests but did not attend. At the head of the table was a *noble baron of beef;* the Ducal Coronet and the banners of the illustrious House of Norfolk were displayed over it. In the evening there was a most brilliant ball. His Grace, dressed in regimentals, opened the ball with the Marchioness of Stafford, and they were followed by about fifty couple. Supper was announced at one o'clock, and on the entrance of the company into the supper rooms, the band of the Sussex Militia struck up " O the roast beef of Old England." The Duke, after the festivities were over, retired to a tent erected for the occasion in the court yard, and here it is supposed he caught a cold, of which he never recovered, for he died the 16th. of December following, being in the sixty-ninth year of his age.

The Drawing Room

Or State Chamber contains many original and valuable portraits of the Earls of Arundel and Dukes of Norfolk, in nearly a complete series.

There is also a fine historical piece, whose subject is the Earl of Surrey vindicating his conduct to Henry VII. for taking part with Richard III. Princess Elizabeth, whom Henry married, who was sister to the young princes who were smothered in the tower, is seen in the back ground displaying the red rose in token of the union of the late rival houses of York and Lancaster.

At the south end of this magnificent apartment is a large window of stained glass, painted by ***Eginton*** of Birmingham, representing the late Duke and Duchess as King Solomon and the Queen of Sheba at a banquet. This window gives the room a splendour and dignity beyond conception. At the opposite end is an orchestra, and over the door an exquisite imitation of basso relievo, by Le Brun, the subject of which is Adam and Eve in Paradise.

The Marshal's Bed and Dressing Rooms may be noticed for an elaborately carved mahogany four post bedstead, with furniture of crimson damask. The hangings also are crimson to correspond.

The Prince of Wales's Apartments consist of a noble bed room and dressing room. The bedstead has eight posts of mahogany, carved in an exquisite stile; the furniture of rich cut velvet. The stools and dressing tables are covered with the last mentioned costly material, and the apartments are both hung with silk tapestry of the richest workmanship.

In the Breakfast Room are two paintings by Hogarth, the one a view of the castle in its ancient state, the other a representation of Covent Garden Market, belonging to the Dukedom.

The Apartments of the Empress Maud when she came to claim the crown in 1139, are situated in the tower above the old gateway, and consisted of the bed rooms, in which she remained when King Stephen laid seige to the castle. There are niches in the wall, near the great sliding door (which protected the entrance to these apartments) which appear to have been intended for centinels. The late Duke of Norfolk intended to have the subterraneous passage explored, and the well also searched, in order to discover whether there were deposited some of the valuable treasures of its former illustrious possessors, during the various periods of intestine tumults that have agitated the country; but the death of that nobleman prevented the undertaking from being accomplished. The well is supposed to be three hundred feet deep.

The Collegiate CHURCH of Arundel,

Was founded by Richard, Earl of Arundel, in 1387, pursuant to the will of his father. Though dissolved at the Reformation, it was granted by patent to Henry, Earl of Arundel, the patron.

Of the original buildings there are considerable remains. The scite was upon an eminence opposite to the western ditch of the castle. The master's house stood at the east end of the chapel, open to the church yard. The other sides were occupied by the apartments of the fraternity. As the chapel was intended to be the chief burying place of the founder's successors, every preparation was made for its future monumental splendour, and the tomb of Thomas, Earl of Arundel, his son, was the first of a very noble series. The present dilapidated appearance may be traced partly to the violence committed by Cromwell's soldiers during the seige of the castle in 1643-4, and partly to age, lastly to ruinous neglect, when the roof of timber frame, richly painted and gilt, was removed in 1782, and was suffered to fall in large fragments upon the tombs. The windows were all filled with stained glass. The eastern contained a series of kneeling figures male and female, in coat armour and mantles of their respective bearings. By the whole a series of portraits of the Earls and Countesses of Arundel were formed. All were broken in pieces by Waller's soldiers. Fresco paintings of arms and cognizances covered the side walls, The high altar, which appears like a very large table tomb covered by a slab of Sussex marble is still entire. Divided by low arches on the north side stands an additional sepulchral chapel, erected for the reception of a chantry in memory of John Fitz Alan, Baron Maltravers, by Elizabeth, his widow, daughter of Sir John Berkeley.

At the dissolution, the scite and buildings of the College, with the exception of the sepulchral chapel and the master's lodgings, suffered immediate and considerable dilapidation.

The Church was dedicated to St. Nicholas, and is supposed to have been built about the year 1380, by Richard, the third Earl of the Fitz Alan family, in consequence of the decay of the collegiate church. He resolved to rebuild it entirely upon new and enlarged foundations, and to connect it in one structure with the chapel of his college, then about to be established. The church, both in point of dimensions and architectural proportion, is not exceeded by any in the district. The pulpit is of carved stone, at the south-eastern angle of the nave, such as are frequently seen in large churches of this era of architecture.

MONUMENTS now remaining.

1. A large sculptured table tomb, (in the centre of the choir,) composed of alabaster formerly painted and gilt, of Thomas, Earl of Arundel, son of the founder, and Beatrix his wife. At the feet a sculptured horse, (the Fitz Alan cognizance) and two dogs usually placed on the tombs of women of high rank.

2. A plain altar tomb of Sussex marble in memory of John, Lord Maltravers, who died the 21st. of April, 1421, as appears by the inscription.

3. An open bier carved in alabaster, under which an emaciated naked figure is extended on a shroud. The head is supported by two angels. It represents John Fitz Alan, to whom the Earldom of Arundel was confirmed, and who was slain at the battle of Gerberoy, in 1432.

4. A large and lofty sacellum, composed of very beautiful tabernacle work in alabaster, originally richly painted and gilt, erected to the memory of Thomas, Earl of Arundel, Baron Maltravers and Clunne, who married Lady Margaret, "one of the eyres of Richard Wodevyle, Earl Rivers, sister to Elizabeth, Queen of England, some time wife to King Edward IV." and to William, Earl of Arundel and Maltravers.—The design and workmanship resemble the tomb of Lord La War at Boxgrove.

5. A tomb erected for William, Earl of Arundel, and his Countess, daughter of Henry, Earl of Northumberland.

Every lover of architecture must deeply lament the disgraceful dilapidated state in which the chancel of this venerable structure is suffered to remain, to which some of the finest specimens of gothic architecture in the county must shortly fall a prey.

The chapel over St. Mary's Gate, now leading into the park, was founded and endowed under the will of Thomas, Earl of Arundel, who died in 1416. The gateway was nearly dilapidated when it was rebuilt by the late Duke of Norfolk in its original state.

CHAPTER XV.

LITTLEHAMPTON.

The route is through Felpham, over a new road lately made by virtue of an Act of Parliament, which reduces the distance from Bognor, its sister watering place, to about seven miles. You cross the River Arun by means of a ferry boat, of very curious description, the motion of which is almost imperceptible, and the passage is effected in about two or three minutes. The town of Littlehampton, from its proximity to the sea, and to the busy River Arun, is a flourishing thriving place, particularly since, by means of the ferry, and the shortening of the road, a more easy access is afforded to Bognor. The town is at a distance from the lodging houses, which are rather too much exposed to the sea.

A new and very handsome church has lately been erected at Littlehampton, to which the society for erecting churches very liberally contributed, and the remainder of the expence was raised partly by the sale of pews and partly by subscription. The soil of Littlehampton is amongst the best on the coast.

CHAPTER XVI.

BIGNOR ROMAN REMAINS.

The route to a visit to these valuable and interesting remains of antiquity is through Bersted, Shripney, and Westergate, and thence into the Arundel road. Turn off immediately opposite the *Ball's Hut* public house, through Fair Mile Bottom, and proceed to the top of Bury Hill, where a fine burst of country opens to the view; of immense and diversified extent. Amberley Castle, the ancient seat of the Bishops of the diocese, but now converted into a comfortable farm house, and Parham Park, the residence of The Honorable Robert Curzon, are seen distinctly on the right, and Chichester and the hills of Hampshire, with the Isle of Wight on the left. At the bottom of Bury Hill is a small public house, and nearly opposite is a lane leading to Bignor.

The discovery was made in the summer of 1811, by a ploughman as he was ploughing the field. The fact being made known to the Duke of Norfolk, he and the neighbouring antiquarians became deeply interested. At first only a small space, covered with tesselated pavement, was exposed to view; but on clearing the ground other discoveries were made. In the second volume of Mr. Dallaway's History of Sussex is contained a learned dissertation on these remains, which is of too classical a character for general readers in a work like this. We shall therefore select from a modern publication the following account of those specimens of ancient grandeur.

At the western side of the field is found that portion of the pavement which is least perfect. The roots of trees which once grew in the adjacent hedge are supposed to have injured it; and the grubbing of those roots nearly completed its destruction. However there are still remaining the figures of a pheasant, of a porpoise, and of the head of a female. Beneath the porpoise are the letters T. R. The female is apparently intended to represent winter, as she is covered to the chin with thick clothing, and holds a leafless branch.

Extending from thence eastward, runs the floor of what has been termed the chrypto porticus, which is supposed to reach upwards of fifty yards. This passes to the south of that pavement which was first discovered and which is now found to be the floor of a large room thirty-two feet in length and thirty feet in its greatest breadth. The south side of this room contains an hexagonal basin of stone, which has generally been called a bath, but on the use of which antiquarians are not agreed. On the *outside* of the stone work it measures six feet from any angle to its opposite, but *within* only four feet: the depth is only nineteen inches; so that it scarcely could have been used for a bath for any other purpose than washing the feet. The basin is surrounded by a pavement exhibiting figures of men and women in various attitudes, not in a very perfect state. Detached ornaments of different kinds are found in the intervals of the figures; and the whole is bounded at the side by a deep Grecian border of black tessalæ on a white ground. The pavement, as well as the room, is contracted in breadth towards the north, and in that part is seen, in fine preservation, the Eagle of Jupiter, bearing away Ganymede, the shepherd of Mount Ida. This is surrounded by a circular serrated border, and other concentric circles. The outer pattern of the pavement here is square, and the interval between the circular boards and the outside is filled up with diamond shaped figures*.

From the Eagle and Ganymede, a passage with mosaic floor leads towards the west. There is nothing remarkable in this part of the pavement except its excellent state of preservation. It consists merely of diamond-like figures and other straight lined ornaments.

Near the end of this passage is another room, the chief part of which is in fine preservation, and of beautiful workmanship. This room is thirty-one feet long and eighteen in width. Its form is that of a rectangle, terminating in a semicircle at the northern extremity. Within the semicircle is a fine head of Juno, exhibiting all the ideal beauty and commanding dignity of the Queen of Heaven. A peacock attends her on each side. This semicircle contains a beautiful spiral border, executed in the most tasteful manner. Beneath the head of Juno and its surrounding ornaments a breadth of the west exhibits four pair of armed gladiators: some actually engaged; others preparing for the fight; and one wounded and struck to the ground,

* In Mr. Dallaway's second volume is an elegant coloured engraving of this part of the remains.

apparently about to perish by the uplifted sword of his adversary. Accompanying the combatants are four unarmed attendants, whose occupation seems to be to prepare them for the battle. The gladiators form a most interesting portion of this truly admirable pavement. The centre of this room is unfortunately broken up, but the southern end exhibits several figures in the attitude of dancing, and is terminated by a handsome border. This room alone is extremely well worth the attention of the curious, whether conversant in antiquity or not. No person can behold for the first time, without feeling a high degree of pleasure and astonishment, this fine specimen of the taste and workmanship of the ancient masters of the world.

In the adjoining field have been discovered a Medusa's head, and part of a bath lined with coloured mortar. The rooms contain no fire places, but were warmed by fires on the outside, whence the heat was conveyed by flues carried under the floors and into the walls. In the Juno room these flues are now visible, and some of the cinders still remain. In the flues are several large thin Roman bricks. Portions of stone pillars have been dug up and one or two coins.

The whole now appears to much greater advantage than when it was first discovered, Mr. Tupper, in whose field these remains are, having, by the recommendation of a learned antiquary, covered the pavement with rooms, the foundations of which are erected precisely on those of the old Roman walls.

The pavements are composed of minute cubical bricks or tessalæ of various colours, grey, black, white and red, the side of each measuring about half an inch. These are sometimes intermixed in the figures with small greenish glass. It is wonderful that the pavements, composed of such materials, should have preserved their beauty for so many centuries. The Romans have now left England fourteen hundred years, and it is not improbable that these pavements were laid down many years before that time, and probably soon after the Romans had established themselves in absolute power in Britain. The Roman road from Chichester ascends the South Downs, at the distance of about a quarter of a mile; at the top of the hill it assumes the name of the Devil's Bank.

A pavement of such costly workmanship is, with reason, supposed to have been the scite of the villa of a Roman general, and the supposition derives an increase of probability from the situation of Bignor, which stands in a central position with respect to the military stations of the Romans at Pulborough, that of Ford near Arundel, and their grand establishment at Chichester. Indeed it is the opinion of a learned antiquary that Bignor was the Roman station designated in the Iter of Richard of Cirencester by the words "*Ad Decimum**," at the tenth mile stone, a description which nearly corresponds with its actual distance from Chichester, the Roman Regnum.

The following is an account furnished by Mr. Elmes the Architect, who states that there has not been for many years so important a discovery of the actual state of the fine arts among the Romans in Britain as this.

"The field in which this important discovery was made lies in the valley under Bignor Hill,

*Page 154 of Mr. Hatcher's ed. 1809. Iter xv.

about a quarter of a mile from the Roman road, which is described in the Iter of Richard of Cirencester, which lies nearly in a direct line from the summit of Bignor Hill to Chichester. The portion of the bath which is discovered is a beautiful tesselated pavement of Mosaic work, in a high state of preservation. In the centre of a circle, fourteen feet in diameter, bordered with two concentric lines, and a twisted scroll between them, formed by black, white, grey and red cubes, is an hexagonal vapour bath, with steps down to it four feet wide from each angle to its opposite, in the centre of which is a leaden pipe or caliduct. The bath is formed of free stone, and the surrounding pavement of cubes of pottery, and a semi-diaphanous glass. This large circle is divided round the hexagonal compartments of a similar size, bounded with a scroll border, and having without that another of rectangular fret work. In the centre of each of these appears a Bacchante, with floating drapery, executed in bold stile—the drawing of which is extremely correct; the colours are fresh, and the figures have elegance, grace and variety. The large circle is bounded by a square of black lines, and the spandrels are fitted with the vase or amphora of Bacchus, and decorated with vine leaves; and to the east are the remains of what evidently went all round it, a large external border of rectangular frets. At the north end is a smaller circle of eight feet diameter, bounded with three inch borderings of a fret, and intertwined scroll of radii of black and white cubes. In the centre is a well executed eagle flying off with Ganymede, a most graceful floating form, with his Phrygian cap, crook, and Grecian sandals. At about fifty yards from this is a smaller fragment of beautiful fret work, a small well executed dolphin, and the initials of T. R. These discoveries are not much more than fifteen or sixteen inches below the earth, the whole of which abounds in fragments of Roman pottery, stones, and plaisters; and from the remains of a capital, probably of one of the columns of the superstructure, I conjecture it to have been executed in the declining times of the Roman Empire, being a compound debasement of the Roman Doric, of cimæ reverse in the abacus, and a colarino nearly two thirds of diameter below it. The Rev. Mr. Douglas, an antiquary of deserved celebrity, conjectures it to have been the remains of a villa of a Roman Prætor, who had the care of the sea-coast about the time of Theodosius. A. D. 397.

A particular account of this Roman Villa has been published in the eighteenth volume of the Archæologia, written by J. Lysons, Esq. V. P. of the Society of Antiquaries of London, and read to that Society the 17th June, 1813, and 9th March, 1815. That celebrated antiquarian is of opinion that the general stile and arrangements of the ornaments which uniformly prevail in all these pavements, differ from any yet discovered in Britain, and have the appearance of much greater antiquity. The figures too, he says, are composed of much better materials, and are much better drawn and executed than those which appear in other works of the kind so frequently found in this island: and by a comparison of the different specimens of Mosaic work discovered at Bignor, with the figures of similar remains in other parts of Europe, the age of which has been pretty satisfactorily ascertained there appears good grounds for supposing that they may be referred to as early a period as the reign of Titus Vespasian, who began his reign in the seventy-ninth year of the christian era;—and consequently that they are upwards of seventeen hundred and fifty years old. No visitor therefore should fail of inspecting these valuable remains of antiquity.

BIGNOR! adieu—*They* little thought who till'd
From year to year, in many an age thy field;
Who gleaned, in merry mood, its golden store,
The surface hid the proud patrician's floor!
That here, once met the conquerors of the world;
And, at the British chief, defiance hurled.
That here, the war-horse tramped to martial sound,
And ensigns wav'd, and cohorts bright were found.
When falling Rome called back each warlike son,
To stay the vengeance of the daring Hun,
And check the barbarous nations of the North,
That from their sterile realms had issued forth,
To spread the wrecks of war around the plain,
Where peace, and smiling joy, were wont to reign;
Cimmerian darkness came o'er Britain's isle,
The arts were banished—and each splendid pile
That Roman luxury had raised, became
A heap of ruins, and unknown to fame.—
A PEASANT'S PLOUGH restored these glories bright,
And thousands thronged astonished at the sight!

TO THE OWERS LIGHT, OFF BOGNOR.

Beam on thou beanteous beacon-light,
Thou seeming sea-star of the night;
Beam on—lest some lone mariner
On the rude rocks thou lightest there
Should shatter his benighted bark,
Without thy lamp to cheer the dark.
Beam on—and may to-morrow's sun
View the sea wanderer's voyage done,
Restored his home—his haven won!
Thus Reason lends her sparkling light,
To point the wrong to show the right;
Thus Virtue holds her torch of truth
To gild our age—to guide our youth;
Thus shows how unreal, how thin,
The specious veil that covers sin;
Tells us where dangers depths are nigh;
Points where the rocks of evil lie;
And warns us, if we strike, we die!
Thus, too, Religion's rarer ray
Lights us poor pilgrims on our way,
Hanging her lamp of holiness,
Our steps to guide—our paths to bless;
And throwing all her lustre out,
To cherish faith, and banish doubt!
O, may we see the lights they've given,
And may our voyage end in HEAVEN!

INDEX OF DISTANCES FROM TOWN TO TOWN.

The names of the respective towns are on the top and side of the square: where both meet gives the distance.

	Arundel	Battle	Brighton	Chichester	Cuckfield	East Bourne	East Grinstead	Hailsham	Hastings	Horsham	Lewes	Midhurst	Petworth	Rye	Shoreham	Steyning	Uckfield	Winchelsea	Worthing	Distance from London.
Arundel																				59
Battle	53																			56
Brighton	20	33																		52
Chichester	11	64	31																	61
Cuckfield	24	38	14	35																39
East Bourne	42	18	22	53	32															60
East Grinstead	37	34	27	47	13	31														29
Hailsham	40	14	21	52	26	7	26													59
Hastings	60	8	40	71	46	18	42	20												64
Horsham	22	50	20	30	12	43	18	39	54											36
Lewes	28	25	8	38	14	18	21	13	34	26										50
Midhurst	12	62	29	12	28	51	36	50	70	21	37									50
Petworth	11	59	23	14	24	46	33	44	64	16	31	5								49
Rye	71	15	51	81	53	30	48	29	11	66	40	77	72							63
Shoreham	15	39	6	26	19	28	32	27	46	20	14	27	26	57						56
Steyning	14	45	12	25	12	34	25	33	51	14	20	22	17	63	6					50
Uckfield	26	26	17	48	13	21	13	13	33	25	9	40	35	42	23	25				41
Winchelsea	69	13	49	79	51	28	46	27	9	64	38	75	70	2	55	61	40			64
Worthing	9	45	12	20	21	34	34	33	52	20	20	20	20	63	6	9	29	61		56

FINIS.

www.ingramcontent.com/pod-product-compliance
Ingram Content Group UK Ltd.
Pitfield, Milton Keynes, MK11 3LW, UK
UKHW022356150425
5479UKWH00061B/93

9 781019 436851